sorted

sorted

Taming Wicked Problems with Smart Leadership Skills

Clive Smallman PhD

GRAMMAR
FACTORY
— EST⁰ 2013 —

Published by Grammar Factory Publishing,
an imprint of MacMillan Company Limited.

Grammar Factory Publishing
MacMillan Company Limited
25 Telegram Mews, 39th Floor, Suite 3906
Toronto, Ontario, Canada
M5V 3Z1

www.grammarfactory.com

Smallman PhD, Clive
Sorted: Taming Wicked Problems with Smart Leadership Skills.

Paperback ISBN 978-1-998756-10-0
Hardcover ISBN 978-1-998756-12-4
eBook ISBN 978-1-998756-11-7

1. BUS019000 BUSINESS & ECONOMICS / Decision-Making & Problem
Solving. 2. BUS071000 BUSINESS & ECONOMICS / Leadership. 3.
BUS041000 BUSINESS & ECONOMICS / Management.

Cover design by Designerbility
Interior layout design by Setareh Ashrafologhalai
Book production and editorial services by Grammar Factory Publishing

Grammar Factory's Carbon Neutral Publishing Commitment

Grammar Factory Publishing is proud to be neutralising the carbon
footprint of all printed copies of its authors' books printed by or ordered
directly through Grammar Factory or its affiliated companies through
the purchase of Gold Standard-Certified International Offsets.

contents

'Houston, we've had a (wicked) problem'

Apollo 13, 1970

On 11 April 1970, astronauts Jim Lovell, Jim Swigert and Fred Haise were 330,000 kilometres from Earth in the command and service module (CSM) of Apollo 13, on their way to land on the Moon [1]. Back in Houston, Mission Control asked Swigert to perform a routine process to stir the oxygen tanks, which were vital to power the CSM and ensure the crew had breathable air.

One and a half minutes after Swigert threw the switch, there was a 'pretty large bang', as he described it. The CSM's electrical power fluctuated, and the module's positional thrusters fired. Communications with and tracking by Earth were broken for a little under two seconds. Lovell looked out the window and saw 'a gas of some sort' venting out of the capsule.

After re-establishing contact with Mission Control, Lovell uttered the famous phrase: 'Ah, Houston, we've had a problem.'

If you watched the ensuing drama live on television at the time—or saw the 1995 movie starring Tom Hanks—you'll recall what happened. As was revealed later, Swigert's routine maintenance action ignited damaged wire insulation inside the CSM's oxygen tanks, causing an explosion that vented the contents of both tanks into space. The CSM's propulsion and life support systems could not operate without oxygen; there was no replacement for the oxygen; and resources for return to Earth were limited.

At that point, however, no one in the CSM or back at Mission Control knew the true extent of the damage—all anybody knew was that Apollo 13 was at risk, the crew's lives were at stake, and they were hundreds of thousands of kilometres away from home, in the black vacuum of space.

THREE YEARS LATER, Horst Rittel and Melvin Webber, a pair of design theorists working at the University of California, Berkeley, would define a term that encapsulated what the endangered astronauts and their support team on the ground had been facing. The Apollo 13 mission hadn't just had a problem, but a *wicked* problem.

Why 'wicked'?

So what are 'wicked' problems? Although they do possess some characteristics associated with the classical idea of evil—in that they threaten the common good, and some may indeed have a moral dimension to them—they are defined as problems:

- that exist in *open systems*, i.e., processes, entities or subsystems that interact dynamically with their environment, and which continuously evolve and adapt due to a multiplicity of variables and stakeholders;

- whose root causes are challenging to define;

- have lots of interacting sub-problems (some obvious, others not);

- involve multiple stakeholders, who may struggle to agree on how to rank the relative urgency of those sub-problems;

- have no single solution; and

- are only partially or temporarily resolvable.

That above definition may sound a little anodyne, but when you start fleshing it out with examples, you begin to realise the sometimes terrifying scale of what we're talking about here. If the wicked problem of the Apollo 13 mission threatened three human lives, the wickedest problems—such as the climate crisis, war, terrorism, pandemics or mass refugee migrations[1]—multiply that number exponentially. These problems bring widespread disorder and chaos, and they can damage or destroy people, property, businesses, and even the planet itself. (To give one particularly infamous example, the asteroid strike that instigated the demise of the dinosaurs was undoubtedly a wicked problem—and, lest we forget, asteroids continue to be an existential threat to life on Earth.)

---

1 See https://www.wicked7.org/what-is-a-wicked-problem/ accessed 22 June 2022

Before we overload our brains (and emotions) with wicked problems of such cataclysmic scale, however, let's consider something a little more reassuring—namely, the fact that since we have taken the time to conceptualise these potentially destructive forces, we have also long been strategising ways to deal with them.

As noted above, the concept of wicked problems was first popularised in 1973 by the Berkeley design theorists Rittel and Webber. They, in turn, were building on the work of Nobel laureate Herbert Simon, an artificial intelligence pioneer, economist and organisation scientist who had first outlined what he referred to as 'ill-structured problems' in 1969 [2].

Rittel and Webber defined 'wicked problems' thus [3]:

1 Problems that are not easily and certainly nor definitively formulated.

2 Unless they run out of 'fuel' (of whatever sort), they don't stop.

3 Their 'solutions' are not true or false, but good or bad.

4 It is difficult to immediately or ultimately test a 'solution'.

5 Every 'solution' is a 'one-shot operation'—there is no opportunity to learn by trial and error, and every attempt counts significantly.

6 They do not have an enumerable set of potential 'solutions', nor is there a well-described set of permissible operations.

7 They are essentially unique.

8 They are sometimes a symptom of another problem.

9 The choice of explanation determines the nature of the problem's 'resolution'.

10 The problem-'solver' has no right to be wrong.

You'll notice that in Rittel and Webber's list, words like 'solve' and 'solution' are always in speech marks. This is because of what is perhaps the most defining characteristic of wicked problems, which is:

We can never solve wicked
problems, only tame them.

The wickedest aspect of wicked problems is that they resist any final, fixed resolution. Like that killer cyborg in *The Terminator*, most often a wicked problem simply *will not stop*, and will always be back in some form. This is why, at best, we can only ever *tame* wicked problems, which is rather akin to herding cats—you can never ultimately succeed, but you may at least get some of them moving in the direction you want.

To give you an example of a wicked problem being tamed, let's briefly return to the story of Apollo 13.

With the CSM's oxygen leaking into space, Mission Control cancelled Apollo 13's planned lunar landing and set a new mission objective—bringing the crew home alive.

As the first step, the crew shut down the CSM's systems to conserve its remaining resources, and then transferred into the ship's landing module, which was equipped with enough oxygen to support two men for two days. Mission Control then improvised new procedures that would stretch that allowance to support three men for four days, allowing the module to function as a 'lifeboat'.

Nevertheless, the crew still experienced considerable hardship, with limited power, a chilly, wet cabin, and a shortage of drinking water. Moreover, they had no assurance that Mission Control's plan to 'slingshot' the ship around the Moon to provide it with enough velocity to return to Earth would work.

As we know, Apollo 13's crew ultimately did return safely. However, while we can rightfully celebrate the ingenuity and dedication of both the crew and their team at Mission Control, their success came not from *solving* the problem of the damaged spacecraft. Rather, they *tamed* it such that its danger was minimised as far as possible, to the point that it both literally and metaphorically ran out of fuel.

Wicked organisational problems

As we've seen, wicked problems can manifest them-selves in many ways and on any scale—from a mal-function that imperilled the lives of three men, to a cataclysmic cosmic event that wiped out an entire spe-cies (the dinosaurs). But for the purposes of this book, we're going to narrow our view to the field in which I've primarily studied the phenomenon of wicked problems over my thirty years as a risk and crisis management specialist: organisations and businesses.

Wicked organisational problems have existed for as long as there have been organisations, and many of them remain common today. As Christine Pear-son and Ian Mitroff note, wicked problems routinely faced by organisations include such things as [4]:

- environmental accidents,
- hostile takeovers,
- sexual harassment,
- health and safety failures,
- product recalls,
- industrial espionage,
- reputational damage, and more.

However, in the last several years we seem to have witnessed a marked increase in both the frequency and severity of these problems, with the COVID-19 pandemic being only the most evident and large-scale example. Whether this perceived increase is simply a case of these problems now being reported more often than they used to be, or because our natural, political, economic, social and technical environments truly are becoming more volatile, uncertain, complex and ambiguous—what we in the risk management field refer to as 'VUCA'—the cold, hard fact is this: wicked problems are here, they're multiplying, and they need to be tamed.

As a leader, you've doubtless encountered and had to deal with your share of wicked problems already (and if you're one of the lucky ones that haven't, believe me, you'll have to at some point!). However, the unfortunate truth is that for every new one that crops up, you'll have to reckon with the seventh point on Rittel and Webber's list: that *every wicked problem is unique*. What this means is that, no matter how well you may have tamed the wicked problems you've had to face previously, you will never be able to use that prior experience to devise a one-size-fits-all solution—because, of course, if there *were* such a solution, the problem wouldn't be wicked in the first place.

On top of that, here's another cold, hard truth:

> Organisations are comprised of individuals, and it's people who have to fix wicked problems, not the organisation.

By their very nature, successful organisations are built on the premise of predictability and standard-isation, which are two of the qualities that wicked problems innately defy. So when these problems arise, it's the human qualities of intuition, analysis, improvisation and decisiveness that have to be brought to bear to adequately tame them—but those laudable traits are bound up with the equally human doubts, flaws and failings that can work to prolong or even exacerbate wicked problems.

So, what are some of these individual traits and behaviours that can perpetuate the struggle of dealing with wicked problems? They include:

- **Uncertainty.** It can be challenging to even adequately define and describe the wicked problem we're facing, and also to determine the ideal outcome of taming it.

- **Fear of failure.** We worry that the problem is so complex or chaotic that our standard problem-solving methods won't work, so we are loath to step up and tackle it because we might not live up to others' expectations.

- **Ego.** Our self-perception about our position or reputation within the organisation can override our ability to think critically, which is essential for dealing with wicked problems.

- **Perfectionism.** We can focus too much on developing a 'perfect' solution before taking actual action on a wicked problem, when the urgency of the situation demands that we get moving equipped with only a sketch.

- **Complacency.** We may devise a solution and declare, 'That's it'; but wicked problems tend to evolve, and our 'solution' may soon be moot.

There are doubtless many more factors we could add to that list, but you get the idea. So the question is—burdened as we are with these all-too-human infirmities—what do we *do* when confronted with the daunting complexity and chaos of wicked problems?

This is the very challenge I've spent my last thirty years or so facing as a specialist in risk and crisis management. I've mentored, coached and trained all sorts of people in all types of businesses and organisations of all sizes, and walked alongside them as they sought to tackle the wicked problems that plagued their fields, as well as the challenging opportunities. And, based on that experience and observation, I've sought to equip entrepreneurs, founders, owners and leaders with a set of principles that will better allow them to tame wicked problems and take advantage of wicked opportunities, on both an individual and organisational scale.

What do we do when faced with wicked problems? We get SORTED.

Sorted: Taming wicked problems with smart leadership thinking

What does 'sorted' mean?

In brief, it's London slang for having your life in order—or, in other words, 'having your s**t together'. In my mentoring practice, though, I expand that idea into six principles—SORTED—to give a more definite idea of how organisations and leaders can get their s**t together so that they're better equipped to handle wicked problems when they arise.

SITUATION—**Identify your wicked problem** through sharpening your *situation awareness*, developing *deep understanding*, and being attuned to the *weak signals* of wicked problems

OBJECTIVE—**Define the outcomes** you want from your chosen 'solution' to your wicked problem

REALITY—**Assess your position** in regards to the problem with dispassionate critical thinking

TEMPLATE—**Devise possible solutions and road maps** by developing checklists

EXECUTION—**Put the most promising solution in play**— bias yourself towards action

DEVELOPMENT—**Analyse the outcome** so you can improve your problem-solving skills and better insulate your organisation from wicked problems in future

SORTED

Equipping leaders to tame wicked individual and organisational problems

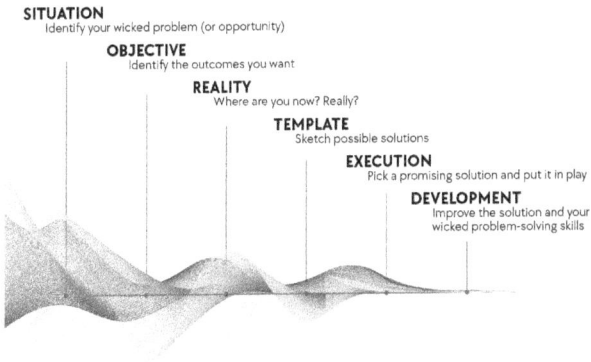

SITUATION
Identify your wicked problem (or opportunity)

OBJECTIVE
Identify the outcomes you want

REALITY
Where are you now? Really?

TEMPLATE
Sketch possible solutions

EXECUTION
Pick a promising solution and put it in play

DEVELOPMENT
Improve the solution and your
wicked problem-solving skills

FIGURE 1 The SORTED Principles

These are the principles that I will lay out for you in the following pages. But first, let me tell you what this book will *not* do.

This book will *not* provide you with some utterly fictional quick fix to eradicate wicked problems, or some fantastical plan to develop an organisation immune to them. From the 'unsinkable' *Titanic*, to the 'impregnable' Maginot Line, to banks that were 'too big to fail', history gives us all too many hubristic examples of supposedly foolproof constructions and institutions that crumbled in the face of wicked problems.

What this book *will* do is something much different. By demonstrating how you can 'sort' yourself to better deal with wicked problems, this book will not simply show you how to make the best of a bad situation. Rather, it will reveal how, through taming wicked problems, you can:

- transform wicked problems into *wicked opportunities* by learning from moments of truth, in order to improve both your own performance and that of your organisation;

- develop a resilient style of leadership—what I call *wicked leadership*—that will optimise and prioritise problem-solving, creativity and innovation; and

- build *reliably safe organisations* by securing consistent financial resources and implementing forward-thinking strategies that enable the organisation to resist, adapt, recover and thrive in the face of changes or challenges over time.

I will go into greater detail about each of these important concepts in the chapters that follow. But, as we get ready to embark on our journey, I want to emphasise that first point as the North Star that we should be following throughout. As I like to say to my clients:

> Beautiful chaos leads
> to wicked opportunities.

We've all heard, and maybe rolled our eyes at, that old cliché, 'For every cloud, there's a silver lining.'

However, when it comes to taming wicked problems, our ultimate success comes when we take them not simply as unwelcome challenges, but as opportunities to learn how we can better navigate our ongoing state of endemic disorder.

In a world of accelerating volatility, uncertainty, complexity, ambiguity, turbulence and contradictions, we can't simply rely on conventional ways of thinking and acting that may have served us in the past. Instead, leaders and organisations need to *embrace* volatility, uncertainty, complexity, ambiguity, turbulence and contradictions as the new foundations for how our world works. They need to shift their models of thinking and adopt a new operating platform that will allow them to function not in perpetual fear of wicked problems, but in the faith that the creative templates we develop to tame them will deliver new ideas and value propositions [3, 5-9].[2]

We must accept that we live not in a state of reliable normalcy that is subject to sporadic disruptions, but rather in a state of perpetual, beautiful chaos. And, by accepting that reality, we can better discover the wicked opportunities that can take our organisations—and our own performance as leaders—to the next level.

So, get your boots on and saddle up. It's time to go out into the wild.

---

2   https://www.fastcompany.com/2682062/turning-wicked-problems-into-wicked-opportunities accessed 22 June 2022

Why Don't We See Wicked Problems Coming?

Hickson & Welch chemical plant explosion, 1992

Early on 21 September 1992, managers at Hickson & Welch, a chemical company located in Castleford, West Yorkshire, in northern England, issued a work order to clean out a chemical reaction tank that had not been cleaned in thirty years. The tank contained nitrotoluene residue, a commonly used but flammable chemical. This sludge was not analysed, and there was no check for flammable vapours in the chamber. The team applied low-temperature steam (under 90 °C) to the tank's base to make the sludge workable. While perched on a scaffold, they used metal rakes to remove the sludge through a manhole in the side of the tank.

At around 1:20 p.m., most of the team stopped working and left for other tasks, leaving only one team member behind. Suddenly, the remaining member saw a blue light that transformed into an orange flame. He quickly jumped to safety as a white-hot, high-speed conical flame shot out of the manhole, followed by a similar jet of fire from the top vent of the tank.

After a moment, the flaming jets subsided, and local fires broke out. The explosive flame destroyed the scaffold, and the adjacent control building was partially burned and bombarded by the manhole cover. The flame also spread to a nearby administration block, causing further fires. Two men died instantly in the control room. In the office block, the fireball severely injured 200 more. A woman and two men died subsequently.

One hundred firefighters, supported by twenty-two fire appliances, had to be called to tackle the incident. The immediate economic cost was £3.5 million (about £7 million at 2023 prices), and the disaster was followed by the shuttering of many local schools, and ultimately the closure of the company itself—to say nothing of the physical and psychic injuries caused to many local families connected to the plant.

N MID-1996, as part of one of my earliest pieces of leadership research, I interviewed the leadership team at Hickson about the 1992 disaster at their plant, with the goal of gathering data about managerial perceptions of risk in particularly high-risk industries. I spoke with eighteen company leaders in total, a group that was uniformly male (not unusual at the time and in that industry) and highly educated, with most having PhDs in chemistry or chemical engineering, mainly from Oxford or Cambridge.

While my interviews with the Hickson team did not ultimately become part of my research writing at the time, I returned to this material thirty years later while researching this book, comparing it against the public reporting of the fire [10]. What I found here—which I will detail later in this chapter—was a cardinal example of the interlocking matrix of *objective* and *subjective* factors that can create a situation in which wicked organisational problems can gestate, and amplify their damage after they manifest themselves.

In the introduction to this book, we established that every wicked problem is unique. However, that does not mean that they are entirely unpredictable, or that we cannot identify certain shared factors that contribute to their manifestation. In the first part of this chapter, therefore, we will examine some of the *general principles* that most wicked problems share, so that we can learn how to spot them.

From there, we move on to the reasons that can prevent us from spotting them—to how our sometimes blinkered *subjective perceptions* of potential risks can keep us from identifying wicked problems until they're suddenly, and potentially disastrously, upon us.

Finally, and most importantly, we will examine the work we can do to help ensure we don't fall victim to that fallacy—namely, by learning how to attune ourselves to the *weak signals* of wicked problems before they emerge, and sharpening our *situation awareness* (as well as that of our organisation itself) so that we can develop a *deep understanding* of our organisational situation.

From 'hot' to 'rip': The objective sources of wicked problems

As we will see when we return to the Hickson tragedy, wicked problems rarely stem from a single, definable source. Rather, they are most often generated from a variety of factors—natural, political, economic, social, technological, etc.—that interconnect in ways that range from simple cause-and-effect to dizzyingly complex.

The work of Paul Shrivastava and his colleagues defined two distinct, interlocking sets of failures that cause wicked problems [11]. The first set comprises the *human*, *organisational* and *technological* factors—or 'HOT' factors—that create the conditions for disorder and lead to the triggering event for the wicked problem.

- **Human**—e.g., operator or managerial errors; sabotage or terrorism; acts of war

- **Organisational**—e.g., policy failures; inadequate safety resources; deliberate overlooking of unsafe practices and conditions; communication failures; misperceptions of the extent and nature of hazards

- **Technological**—e.g., faulty design or procedures; defective equipment; contaminated materials or supplies

These factors then interact with the second set of failures: the *regulatory*, *infrastructural* and *preparedness*—'RIP'—deficiencies in the organisational environment, which enable the triggering event from the HOT factors to escalate into full-blown crises. These failures include:

- **Regulatory**—e.g., weak or complex legislated controls on corporate activities; ineffective or inconsistent enforcement; regulatory capture (where the industry controls the regulator, favouring it over the public interest)

- **Infrastructure**—e.g., lack of monitoring and surveillance capacity; inadequate essential services (water, electricity, transportation, communication)

- **Preparedness**—e.g., inadequate on- and off-site emergency plans; lack of emergency medical capacity; ill-prepared civil defence authorities

The Hickson disaster is an archetype of how all these factors combined to produce a particularly destructive wicked problem. The report on the incident by the UK Health and Safety Executive identifies a complex set of interlocking causes, as we can see below [10].

> The decision to clean out the chemical vessel after thirty years of operation indicated inadequate maintenance systems that were compounded by the misclassification of work areas as non-hazardous, leading to the absence of flame-proofing measures.
>
> Additionally, the failure to analyse the sludge and atmosphere inside the vessel before cleaning worsened the situation, as potential ignition sources were not identified and eliminated. The maintenance team inadequately measured the

sludge's temperature, due to the temperature probe's position. As a result, it supplied steam at a higher temperature than intended, possibly leading to increased flammable vapour production.

Furthermore, the control systems' sensors were inadequate. This shortfall was evidenced by the absence of a work permit for raking out the sludge, despite the issuance of two permits for removing the manhole lid and one for closing off the tank inlet. In addition, the team failed to isolate the tank base inlet before work, a poor maintenance practice.

Using a metal rake to clean the sludge from a tank containing flammable vapours is another example of poor maintenance practices. Finally, the location of the occupied buildings was not optimal, leading to human casualties in the adjacent control room and administration block.

While it was the scraping of a metal rake that triggered this wicked problem, the underlying causes that laid the groundwork for this inciting event were far more profound and pervasive. Working from the bottom up of the HOT factors, the HSE's report demonstrated that the fire at the Castleford plant represented:

- a *human* failure, not only on the part of the maintenance workers that triggered the event, but also the leadership that allowed the cascading organisational and technological failures to take root and persist;

- an *organisational* failure, in the inadequate maintenance system and misclassification of work areas; and

- a *technological* failure, in neglecting to analyse the sludge and atmosphere, as well as the use of inappropriate equipment.

What of the RIP factors in the Hickson case? Looking at the HES' report and the then-prevailing legislation, the Castleford fire was possibly exacerbated by:

- a *regulatory failure*, since, while risk assessment was a part of the legislative framework, the comprehensive Management of Health and Safety at Work Regulations, which made explicit requirements for risk assessment, only came into effect in the same year as the disaster (1992);

- *infrastructural failures* because of inadequate measurement equipment and control systems sensors, and the poor location of administrative and production buildings on the site; and

- *preparedness failures* in hazard identification, temperature measurement and maintenance practices.

There was limited culpability for management failures in such cases at the time. Eventually, the courts fined Hickson £250,000, plus £150,000 costs. However, it wasn't until 2007 that the British government passed the Corporate Manslaughter and Corporate Homicide Act, which made it possible for corporations to be found guilty of manslaughter if serious failures in the management of health and safety result in a fatality. Corporations are now potentially liable, identified with gross breaches of reasonable conduct by senior management or the board. There are now unlimited fines and successful prosecutions have since occurred.

In light of legislation like the UK's Corporate Manslaughter and Corporate Homicide Act, a company must take all reasonable steps to understand and mitigate the risks associated with its activities. This involves conducting objective risk assessments and implementing appropriate safety measures. If a serious incident occurs, and it is found that the company failed to adequately manage objective risks, it could be found guilty under the Act.

However, the legislation also implicitly recognises the role of *subjective risk perceptions*, as companies must account for the concerns and perceptions of risk among their employees and other stakeholders. And therein lies a paradox that sits at the very heart of wicked problems.

Risk is always subjective

Why are people so often unable to spot potentially wicked problems on the horizon? Or, even if they are able to, what leads them to either ignore them or downplay their potential severity? The simple fact is that, to a considerable degree,

Our *subjective perception* of risk determines
the seriousness with which we react to and
appraise a potentially wicked problem.

For all the statistics thrown around by professionals like engineers or actuaries when discussing risk,
in everyday life virtually no one appraises risk by cal-
culating a probability; instead, we make a subjective
judgement. For example, in the summer of 2022-
23, a popular swimming beach near where my wife
and I live in Australia was shut down for a few days
after a shark was spotted offshore. Fancying a swim,
we decided to head to another beach on the opposite side of the headland from the closed beach. We
didn't crunch the numbers on recorded shark attacks
before making our decision—instead, we subjectively
determined that the other beach was safe enough.
Other people made different judgements, and stayed
out of the water.

That same essential dynamic applies whether we
are considering a personal choice that may make us
fish food, or an organisation's potential exposure to
risk. For all that chief risk officers tend to frame risk
as something objective and measurable, at the end of
the day it is always an emotional human, with their
own conditioned responses and mental model of the
world, who assesses that risk's severity and determines how (or how not) to respond to it.

At both the personal and organisational level, our subjective perception of risk operates across three dimensions [14-16]:

1 **Interest-induced**—the extent to which we *want to learn more* about a potential problem

2 **Emotion-induced**—our *affective response* to a problem, ranging from fear or anxiety to blithe lack of concern

3 **Relevance-induced**—the extent to which we feel *personally involved in and affected by* a problem

These three dimensions are innately interrelated, and work to amplify each other as they shape our perceptual response to a potential wicked problem, in either direction. On the one hand, what may initially have been a purely academic interest in a wicked problem (if that) may start to elicit a more significant emotional response from us as we gradually come to grasp its potential severity, and to feel that it is more relevant to us because it could negatively impact ourselves and others.

Conversely, if we don't feel that a potentially wicked problem is relevant to us, we are less likely to be interested or emotionally invested in it—even if data suggests that we should be, either now or later. For instance, people living in inland Australia or New Zealand may generally have a far less urgent reaction to the climate crisis than do Pacific Islanders, who are seeing its effects in their daily lives.

To give another example, consider the wildly different perceptions of the attack on the United States Capitol on 6 January 2021, as per the Final Report of the Select Committee that investigated the attack [12]. For some, the insurrection was a righteous action to overturn an instance of (non-existent) electoral fraud. For others, it was a symbolic act of defiance against institutions that the respondents blamed for perceived systemic wrongs. For many more, it was an attempted *coup d'état* and an assault on the most fundamental values of American democracy.

What this attests to is that *different people have divergent views or interpretations when presented with the same information*. This phenomenon is part and parcel of the observer's paradox [13], which holds that all observations are 'indeterminate' because different observers will offer various explanations for a given set of signals. We make judgements and decisions based not on *what* we sense, but *how* our respective mental models interpret those sensations [14].

Hence, when we look at a wicked problem, each of us will have a different perspective based on our model of the world and our view of the context in which we operate—which can sometimes involve multiple perspectives simultaneously, depending on the various roles we occupy (e.g., employee, private citizen, a member of a particular social group or organisation). Furthermore, thanks to our current age of largely friction-free digital communications, those subjective perceptions can quickly spread to regional, national and global levels with breathtaking speed, finding resonance with others whose perceptions align with our own (perhaps blinkered) view of the problem at hand.

This is how subjective perception can not only create the conditions for wicked problems to emerge, but also amplify their damage *after* they manifest themselves. A widening field of skewed subjective perceptions can create a whole array of secondary negative impacts beyond the actual event itself, simply because finding a response that satisfies most people will be exceedingly difficult. And, as we have established, the further one's perceived proximity from a wicked problem, the less likely one is to approach it with the urgency it demands.

This is a primary reason why, as research I have done on this matter shows, so many senior managers seem not to recognise the risks associated with wicked problems until it is too late. It reminds me of a question I was asked when I presented a paper at a conference on risk management while conducting my doctoral research in the early 1990s: 'Can you identify a significant means of improving managerial perceptions of health and safety risk in the chemical industry?' My only half-joking response: 'Move the managing director's office closer to the site of the most hazardous operation.'

CONCLUSION

The Hickson & Welch chemical plant explosion illustrates the tragic consequences of a complex web of failures in human, organisational, technological, regulatory, infrastructure and preparedness dimensions. This disaster serves as a potent example of wicked problems, which are not solely born out of objective factors: subjective perceptions of risk play a crucial role in exacerbating or downplaying them. These subjective perceptions are shaped by such factors as our personal interests, emotional responses, and the perceived relevance of the problem at hand. In the digital age, these perceptions can rapidly spread, creating a feedback loop that further amplifies the divergence between objective reality and subjective perceptions. It is therefore crucial, particularly in high-risk industries, that those in positions of leadership can see and read the situation before them clearly—which brings us to the first principle of getting SORTED.

situation

Scion Capital and the global financial meltdown, 2008

As the founder of the hedge fund Scion Capital, Michael Burry had already shown his predictive abilities when he made a killing by 'shorting' over-valued tech stocks just as the dot-com bubble was about to burst. In 2007, he cross-referenced several strands of seemingly unrelated information to accurately foresee the failure of a real estate bubble built on the questionable lending practices of the US sub-prime mortgage market, which were exacerbated by remarkably asinine financial derivatives engineering. Together, these then-standard operating procedures had left the US housing market and financial services sector horribly yet covertly exposed, sleepwalking towards the edge of a high cliff.

Had Burry not spotted the signals, Scion would have been on the precipice. Instead, he bought heavily into credit default swaps against subprime mortgage derivatives, which led many of his irate investors to try to withdraw their money as the costs of the swaps rose. Burry's foresight was vindicated when the venerable and prestigious US bank Lehman Brothers went bankrupt in September 2008, presaging the entire global banking sector going into freefall.

While a panicked G20 pumped trillions of dollars into banks and the International Monetary Fund, and governments hastily promised banking reforms (which largely failed to materialise), at Scion, Burry pocketed $100 million personally, while his investors took home $700 million.

T HE STORY OF Michael Burry was one of the primary narrative threads of the book (and film) *The Big Short* [15], which chronicled one of the major upheavals of the 21st century—the global financial crisis of 2007-08—through the experiences of the few people who truly saw it coming.

In this story of remarkable foresight and calculated risk-taking, Burry demonstrated a crucial ability that allowed him to see what so many others in the financial world failed to perceive: *situation awareness*. This skill involves having a deep understanding of one's environment, the ability to perceive potential changes and threats, and the capacity to make well-judged decisions based on that understanding, which makes it invaluable in any context where complex systems interact and evolve. And, as wicked problems often involve the most radical extremes of complexity, situation awareness is obviously the first weapon in our arsenal when it comes to grappling with them.

In this chapter, we will learn about how situation awareness works; how it can be actively cultivated and developed at both an individual and organisational level; and how it serves as our foundational 'early warning signal' in the face of an ever more VUCA world and the wicked problems it presents us with.

The 'weak signals' of wicked problems

People are generally pretty good at spotting blatant dangers. This awareness dates back to when our pre-historic ancestors' lizard brains kept their eyes alert for sabre-toothed tigers and other predators. However, on the whole, we're considerably less good at spotting the *weak signals* of impending doom or disaster [16, 17].

What are 'weak signals'? Put simply, they are often unnoticed or overlooked phenomena that are pre-conditions for later crises. For example, while the UN did not officially declare that the world is facing a climate crisis until 2020, as early as 1896 Swedish scientist Svante Arrhenius predicted that atmospheric carbon dioxide concentration changes could cause significant global warming [18], a finding that was seconded by English engineer and inventor Guy Callendar in 1938 [19]. If these weak signals of our current global predicament were there to be read so long ago, why was it only isolated voices such as Arrhenius and Callendar who brought attention to them?

The answer lies in what Barry Turner and Nick Pidgeon term 'cosy normality' [17]—the culturally accepted beliefs and norms that govern how we think and talk about the world and its hazards. It is within the boundaries of these norms that organisations develop their standard operating procedures and codes of practice, as well as their tacit operating heuristics (or 'rules of thumb'). And, if these norms do not permit the serious consideration of wicked problems that fall outside their 'sphere of acceptability', they can get in the way of us perceiving the weak signals of a wicked problem on the horizon.

As with the issue of the innately subjective perception of risk that we covered in the prelude of this book, the above may make it sound as if innate human imperfection is the root cause for why wicked problems are so often not detected until the crisis point is reached. But while that does factor in considerably, remember what we said about wicked problems in the previous chapter—most often, they derive from not one, but a *variety of sources that interconnect and interact*. The same principle holds for the weak signals of those problems: each of them may seem isolated and unrelated to the others, but upon closer examination, we can see that they are profoundly entangled with each other. And the fact that a few people *can* tune in to that interlocking matrix of weak signals to see what they portend is the exception that proves the rule that, most often, the majority of people will not be able to perceive this pattern.

Think back to the anecdote from *The Big Short*. What allowed Michael Burry to correctly read the weak signals of the impending collapse, when so many other financial experts had been blind to them? To some extent, it surely had something to do with gifts that were unique to him in his ability to analyse and interpret data in a (seemingly) unorthodox way, as well as a personality orientation that made him unafraid to take a contrarian view on conventional wisdom, and to put his money (and his investors') where his mouth was.

But it also had much to do with something that is more broadly accessible—a matrix of habits and mindsets that can allow us to perceive wicked problems before they're upon us, so that we can not only insulate ourselves against them, but also potentially turn them to our advantage. This is the subject that constitutes both the final part of this chapter, and the foundation of being SORTED.

Building situation awareness

Let's leave *The Big Short* behind for a moment and consider an arena nearly as perilous as Wall Street: aerial combat. Imagine you're on the final mission in *Top Gun: Maverick*, flying a Boeing F/A-18 Super Hornet with a top speed of 1,915 km/h, with a pair of Russian-made stealth fighters, capable of making somewhere in the neighbourhood of 2,130 km/h, on your tail. With the enemy bogies closing fast, you have considerably less time than Michael Burry had to make the necessary decisions. And if you get them wrong, you won't be bankrupt—you'll be dead, or at best dropping by parachute into hostile territory.

As a combat pilot, you must have an instantaneously accessible mental map of the relationship between your current location and flying conditions; your aircraft's configuration and complex instrumentation; the state of your engines and fuel; your weaponry; the terrain beneath you and your proximity to the ground; *and* your estimation of your enemy's situation in regards to all of these, not to mention keeping the rules of engagement—i.e., where and when you can (and cannot) fire at your enemy—at the back of your mind.

To put it mildly, this is a complex, stressful and rapidly evolving environment, with multiple inputs demanding your attention. In such a situation, the odds that you will fall prey to sensory overload and fatal decision-making errors are nearly through the roof. With what may well be your life on the line, you need to rely on your ability to both process your current context and forecast how that context will develop. This, in a nutshell, is what we mean by the term 'situation awareness' (or SA, for short), that critical yet elusive foundation for successful decision-making.

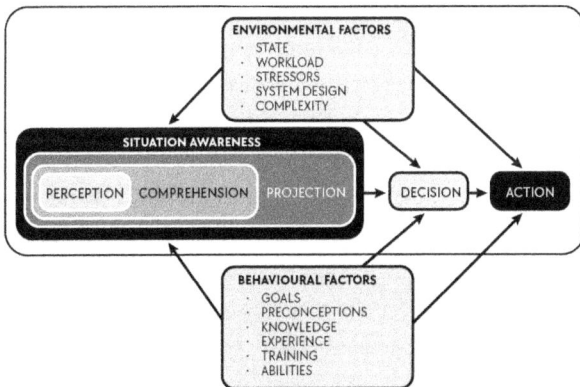

FIGURE 2 Situation awareness

Obviously, the kind of SA you apply in business will almost certainly not be as immediately a matter of life or death as it is to a fighter pilot. But cultivating your ability to assess dangers that may not necessarily be clear and present is vital for both perceiving the potential for wicked problems, and devising ways to tame them—and, possibly, channelling them into wicked opportunities.

In her work on 'dynamic systems', Mica Endsley identifies three key elements of situation awareness: *state*, *systems* and *processes* [20, 21]. Let's take a quick look at each one of these.

State

Our *state* refers to how what is happening inside us governs our awareness of our current situation. It is the dynamic process by which we perceive environmental cues through our senses, process that data through our mental model of the world, and then respond to them by making decisions accordingly [22].

Our state is the foundation of our situation awareness; if our state isn't operating optimally, we are more likely to make poor decisions [23]. This is why it is important that we take active steps to check, maintain and improve this element in our day-to-day lives, the better to keep ourselves alert for those weak signals of wicked problems. Some of these steps include:

Cultivating mindful habits. Learning to focus on the here and now, to leave behind distractions and home in on the immediate space-time we are occupying, allows us to become more aware of our surroundings, thoughts and emotions. This is especially important in the business world, as it allows us to better process information, predict potential risks and opportunities and make more-informed decisions. Engaging in mindful practices like physical exercise and meditation can allow us to decrease our stress levels, enhance our resilience and boost our creativity, enabling us to generate fresh ideas and innovative solutions to complex problems.

Another technique is to find an 'anchor'. Think about a time when you were 'in the zone'—when you were excelling, at the 'top of your game'. Remember how your body felt: your posture, your hands and feet, your face. Recall the data you were receiving from your other senses: what could you see, smell and hear? Once you've recaptured these sensations, *anchor* them by compacting all that feeling into a small physical gesture—e.g., clicking your fingers, or squeezing your thumb and forefinger together. Then, when you falter or find yourself in a challenging situation, use that gesture to return yourself to that feeling, and apply it to the scenario at hand.

Flow is the ultimate state of mindfulness [24]. Also frequently referred to as being 'in the zone' or 'in the groove', it is a state of complete, healthy absorption in an activity. Psychologist Mihaly Csikszentmihalyi first described flow in the 1970s, identifying such characteristics as intense concentration, a sense of control, loss of self-consciousness and a distorted sense of time. In flow, people are focused on the present moment and experience deep satisfaction and enjoyment in the activity.

Flow is often associated with challenging but achievable activities, such as playing a musical instrument, practising a sport or working on a creative project. When we engage in activities that are challenging but within our skill level, we are more likely to experience flow because these activities require our full attention and provide us with immediate feedback on our performance.

Flow has many positive effects on psychological well-being. For example, when we experience flow, we feel more energised, motivated and engaged. In addition, improved performance, creativity and overall satisfaction with life correlate with flow.

Avoiding distractions: Beware of 'shiny objects'. We all face distractions at work every day, sometimes even every hour. Recent research by Udemy [25] shows that 70% of workers feel distracted at work, with 16% feeling they're almost always distracted. Distractions lower our productivity, sap our energy, and work against our situation awareness.

Successfully insulating our state against distractions overlaps with some of the mindful practices we covered above. *Creating a controlled and balanced physical environment* is one useful method. For example, we can seek out a quiet work space, or turn off notifications on our electronic devices.

Staying organised is another helpful practice. We can prioritise our tasks through the use of tools like calendars, to-do lists, project management software, and time-management techniques like the Eisenhower Matrix, which was made famous by Stephen Covey (under the name of 'time management matrix') in *The Seven Habits of Highly Effective People* [26].

We can also ensure that we *have a game plan* for every single day. For example, is there a 'run sheet' for the meeting? Has it been rehearsed with your team? Is there someone who will step up and step in if you're unable to make it in?

In the examples above, we've treated distractions in purely negative terms, as unwelcome intrusions. But there are also distractions that can take on a more insidious form, masquerading as boons, benefits or opportunities. This is what is known as 'shiny object syndrome'—a phenomenon in which leaders are distracted by new, exciting ideas or possibilities that ultimately prove illusory, and can lead to wasted time and resources, and a critical lack of focus and progress on existing projects and goals [27].

To guard against this, leaders need to not only hew to the kind of mindful practices we discussed above, but also make sure that they have *clear, defined business goals* and priorities that *align with the organisation's overall vision and mission*.

Further, so as not to summarily shut the door on innovation and positive risks—because sometimes the glitter on those shiny objects really can be gold—they need to *set boundaries around 'blue-skying' activities*, such as by setting aside specific times for exploring new ideas or opportunities or limiting how much time or money they are willing to invest in these pursuits.

Seeking outside perspectives, from mentors, coaches, advisors or peers, can also be valuable, yielding feedback and guidance on which ideas to pursue and which to avoid.

'Reading the room': Sharpening your social intelligence. As our state is informed by external data as much as by our internal qualities, learning how to understand and relate to other people in our business environment is crucial. In the event of a wicked problem, their reactions will be inextricably bound up with ours; so, if we have familiarised ourselves with the mental and emotional bedrock that determines their reactions, we can better know how to account for or channel these actors in a crisis.

Empathy—the ability to put ourselves in another's shoes, to try to understand their perspective and emotional state—is our 'way in' to this understanding. And, by engaging in *active listening* with our colleagues and collaborators—that is, as per the mindful habits discussed above, being fully present when in conversations—we can not only create stronger relationships with these essential partners, but also perhaps develop and nuance our own perceptions through gaining a deeper understanding of theirs.

Create a workplace culture that reaps you the benefits of others' situation awareness. An organisation can't depend entirely on one leader to help it steer clear of wicked problems. Rather, a leader must cultivate a workplace environment that allows them to channel the aggregate SA of everyone within the organisation to inform their own [28].

Developing a culture that values and benefits from others' situation awareness requires a combination of leadership, communication and collaboration. To begin with, *leaders must model the behaviour they want to see in their team*, by honing and developing their state via the individual-oriented practices of mindfulness we outlined above.

Assembling the right team is also critical for success. *Aim for variety in your team's makeup*, across such categories as hard and soft skills, age, gender, ethnicity and culture. Ensure that they can work together in a spirit of true collaboration, regardless of their respective status, expertise or differing cultural norms.

One way to foster this is to encourage team members from different departments or specialties to work together on projects. This can bring a more productively diverse range of perspectives and insights to bear on the initiative, and help break down silos and barriers to communication within the organisation.

Training and development opportunities are also essential for team members to improve their situation awareness skills. This could include offering courses on effective communication, conflict resolution or decision-making.

Crucially, *all team members must have the capacity for critical thought*. Foster an environment where everyone feels comfortable sharing their observations and insights, even if they contradict the prevailing view. Encourage curiosity and questioning, and clarify that mistakes and failures are opportunities for learning and improvement.

Finally, celebrate instances where team members demonstrate good situation awareness, and use them to drive positive outcomes. This might involve publicly recognising individual or team contributions, or even incorporating examples of good SA in training and development materials.

By laying the groundwork for an inclusive, supportive and collaborative work environment, leaders can amplify their own state by nurturing the state of their team as a whole. When the state of the workforce is optimised, collective situation awareness increases, and leaders can then channel that into better decision-making, improved performance, and a more substantial competitive advantage.

Systems

As we move on to the second keystone of SA, let's return for a moment to the fighter-pilot analogy from earlier in the chapter. Even as aerial combat demands perhaps the highest degree of individual situation awareness we can conceive of, that aviator is not alone: they are part of a complex technological and human *system* that supports virtually every facet of their operation in the air.

As Gene Rochlin and his colleagues detailed in their research on aircraft carrier operations [29], in all naval air operations there is a constant stream of electronic and verbal communication between the aviators and the combat direction centre (CDC). Carrier commanders and operators feed commands, intelligence and information to the pilots, and vice versa. Aircraft computers communicate with ship systems, which upload data to aircraft. In this way, the air combat system *distributes situation awareness between its constituent parts* (the carrier, the aircraft, the crew and the pilots), and *governs information exchange* to enable further decision-making and actions [28].

Similarly, all organisations have a *business model* that allows managers and team members to manage operations effectively by sharing situation awareness across the various elements of the organisation. It is this *system* that activates and channels the aggregate SA of the organisation's collective *state*. Therefore, designing an effective and responsive business model is vital not only for giving your organisation a competitive edge in the market, but also for attuning it to and providing resilience against wicked problems.

There are many approaches to business modelling, but I have found the most useful to be that of Alex Osterwalder and Yves Pigneur [30], whose *Business Model Canvas* breaks organisational operations into nine foundational building blocks.

Once this canvas has been filled in, a *Strategic Planning Framework* for gathering information should be wrapped around it. This framework should include:

- information on *critical trends* in politics, economics, society and culture, technology, and the

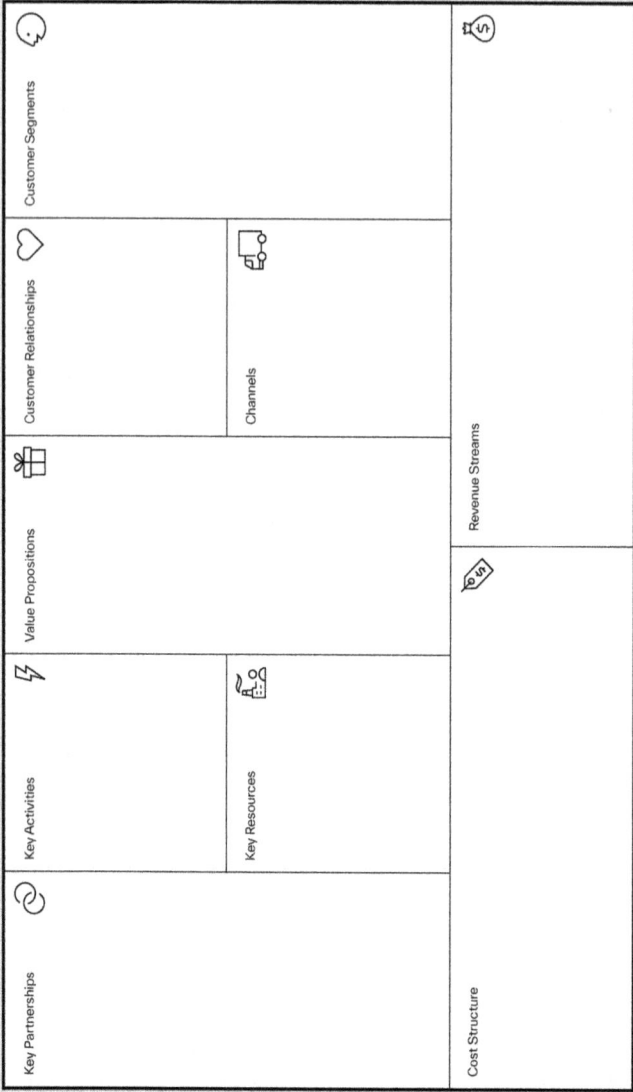

FIGURE 3 The Business Model Canvas. Strategyzer.com

natural environment (commonly referred to as PEST analysis);

- analysis of *market forces* (including segments, needs, demands, market issues, switching costs, market attractiveness and market maturity), as well as *macroeconomic forces* such as global market conditions, capital markets, commodities and other resources; and

- *industry or sector forces*, including buyers, suppliers, stakeholders, incumbent competitors, new entrants and substitute value propositions.

While this conventional strategic framework is essential, it must be supplemented by another vital component of organisational situation awareness—namely, a way to gauge the needs and demands of our customers or clients. And the best way to do this is to develop an *Empathy Map* of each customer segment you serve or intend to serve.

An Empathy Map is a visual tool that helps businesses gain insights into their target audience's experiences, preferences and pain points so that the organisation can better enhance its products, services or communication strategies [31]. As with business models, there are many templates available for creating Empathy Maps, but I like the one developed by XPLANE[3], which is used in the Stanford Design School curriculum and is featured in the *Harvard Business Review*.

---

3   https://xplane.com/worksheets/empathy-map-worksheet/ accessed 24 April 2023

Empathy Map Canvas

Designed for   Designed by   Date: Version:

1 **WHO are we empathizing with?**
Who is the person we want to understand?
What is the situation they are in?
What is their role in the situation?

GOAL

2 **What do they need to DO?**
What do they need to do differently?
What job(s) do they want or need to get done?
What decision(s) do they need to make?
How will we know they were successful?

3 **What do they SEE?**
What do they see in the marketplace?
What do they see in their immediate environment?
What do they see others saying and doing?
What are they watching and reading?

4 **What do they SAY?**
What have we heard them say?
What can we imagine them saying?

7 **What do they THINK and FEEL?**

PAINS
What are their fears,
frustrations, and anxieties?

GAINS
What are their wants,
needs, hopes and dreams?

What other thoughts and feelings might motivate their behavior?

5 **What do they DO?**
What do they do today?
What behavior have we observed?
What can we imagine them doing?

6 **What do they HEAR?**
What are they hearing others say?
What are they hearing from friends?
What are they hearing from colleagues?
What are they hearing second-hand?

Last updated on 16 July 2017. Download a copy of this canvas at http://gamestorming.com/empathy-maps/

© 2017 Dave Gray, xplane.com

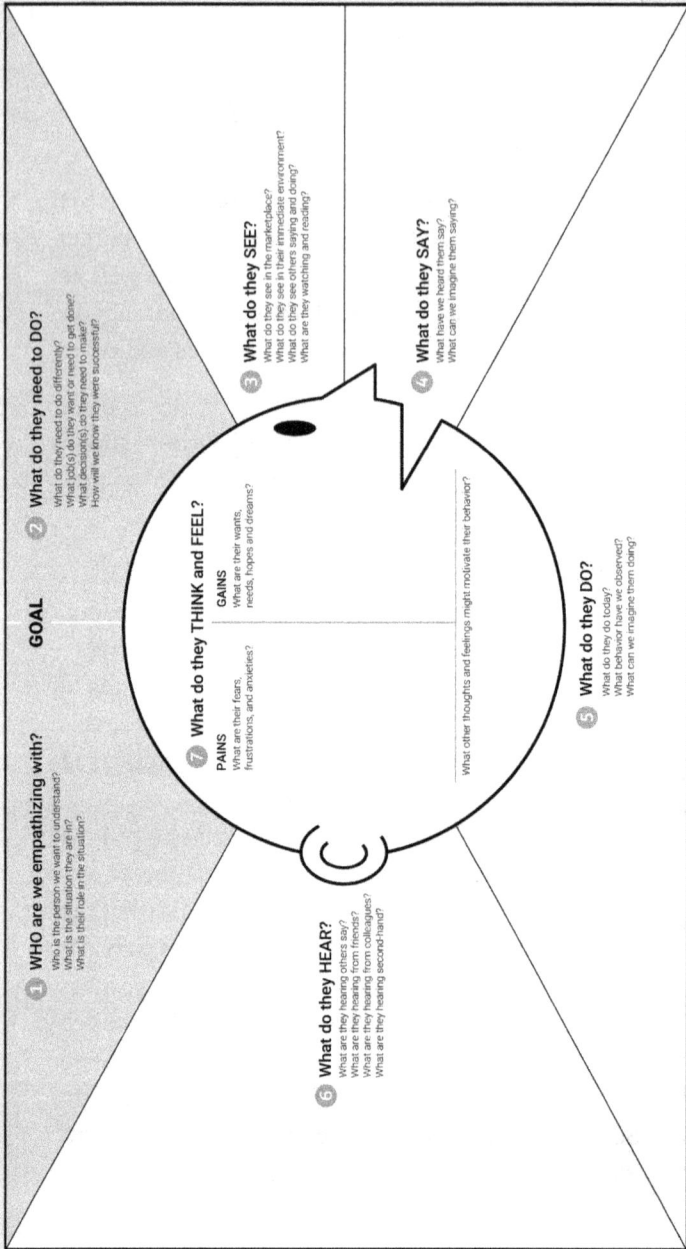

FIGURE 4 Empathy Map. COURTESY OF XPLANE

As you can see in Figure 4, the XPLANE Empathy Map template consists of a seven-segment grid, which we can use to structure the data that we collect through such methods as interviews, surveys, focus groups, social media interactions, etc. By filling out each segment with answers to the questions below, we can build up a profile of the customer segment we wish to target.

AT THIS POINT, you may be saying: 'That's all well and good, Clive, but what does all this business modelling and empathy mapping stuff have to do with wicked problems? Isn't this just basic business know-how?'

On one level, you're absolutely right. Effectively structuring your organisation and knowing your target market are indeed two of the most fundamental rules for any successful business, not a 'break in case of emergency' tool for dealing with the extreme situations presented by wicked problems. But, just as we cultivate our state to serve us in both our regular day-to-day *and* to equip us to perceive and respond to wicked problems, so too must the systems we put in place to manage 'business as usual' also equip us to swiftly respond to wicked problems when they arise.

By working to comprehensively understand the strengths, weaknesses, opportunities and threats within and to our nine organisational building blocks, we are also mapping the broader context in which wicked problems exist, and giving ourselves the space to determine effective solutions to respond to them—

which may demand that one or more of those foundational blocks could have to be radically changed.

To give you an example of how effective business modelling allowed an imperilled organisation to respond to a wicked business problem, let's consider the case of one of the world's most recognisable brands.

CASE STUDY
Lego, 2004–16

In the early 2000s, the Danish toy company Lego, facing stiff competition from a wicked problem bred by advancing technology—the soaring popularity of electronic toys and video games—was on the brink of bankruptcy [32, 33]. In 2004, the company announced its first-ever financial loss, and a significantly reduced market share.

To address these challenges, Lego adopted a new business model that led to a remarkable turnaround. The critical elements of this new model were *innovation*, *simplicity* and *collaboration*.

Realising that it needed to stay relevant in order to attract new customers, Lego established a dedicated innovation team that developed new themes, such as Lego Friends and Lego Ninjago, which were designed to appeal to a broader range of customers.

Lego also invested in digital innovation, developing mobile apps and online games that allowed customers to interact with the brand in new and engaging ways. The company also created a digital design platform called Lego Digital Designer, which allowed customers to design their own Lego sets and share them with others.

The second critical change that Lego made was to simplify its product lines. Previously, the company had been producing hundreds of sets that were often difficult to assemble and had a steep learning curve for younger children. Consciously going against this model, Lego reduced the number of sets it produced and focused on its core product—the basic Lego brick—as well as introducing more flexible pieces that could be adapted to a variety of uses.

Thirdly, Lego established partnerships with other recognised brands, such as Disney and Marvel, to develop Lego sets based on popular movies and characters, and worked with retailers to create in-store displays and promotions to attract customers.

On the customer outreach side, Lego established an online community called Lego Ideas, where customers could submit their own designs for Lego sets and have them voted on by members of the community. Lego then produced the winning designs as actual sets.

This new business model profoundly impacted the company's performance. By 2016, Lego had become the world's largest toy company, with a 26% global market share. In 2017, the company reported revenue of $5.8 billion, an increase of 6% from the previous year.

Lego's transformation was made possible because its system enabled the company to diagnose the wicked problem it was facing, and decisively reposition its core product so that it could fulfil new *kinds* of needs and desires both within and beyond its traditional target market. This is the kind of firm yet flexible system that can successfully deal with wicked problems.

Processes

Within SA, *processes* are the means by which the state of the actors is dynamically interconnected with the systems within which they operate. Within an organisation, there are two primary forms of processes linking you, your colleagues and collaborators, and your supporting, non-human systems. Let's look at each of these in turn.

Contextual SA: Watch the skies. Contextual situation awareness refers to those processes through which you *scan the world in which your organisation operates* to be alert to potential wicked problems [20, 21]. This includes not only an attentiveness to the immediate business environment, but also to the broader social, cultural and historical factors that feed into that environment.

For example, a business looking to market a new product in a foreign country must be aware of cultural differences that may affect how the local population perceives and receives the product. This could involve researching local customs, values and preferences, and understanding the country's political and economic climate.

Operational SA: Watch the ground. Operational situation awareness refers to those processes through which you *scan your organisation's internal workings* to find vulnerabilities that might make the organisation susceptible to wicked problems. This entails being aware of the current status of your systems, the resources available, the constraints under which the organisation functions, and the attendant risks and opportunities all this presents [20, 21].

For example, a company that imports goods from overseas must be aware of potential delays or disruptions in its supply chain due to weather events, port closures or other factors. In addition to regularly monitoring each node in that chain, the company should also have backup plans in place in order to maintain operations in the event of a disruption, such as rerouting shipments or adjusting production schedules.

CASE STUDY
Howard Schultz and Starbucks

When Howard Schultz returned to Starbucks as CEO in 2008, the company was in a dire situation. Its stock price was plummeting, and the company had lost its connection with customers. Schultz was tasked with engineering a turnaround. How aware was he of the circumstances he found himself in?

Firstly, Schultz recognised the current **state** of Starbucks: declining sales, dissatisfied customers and deteriorating brand image. He undertook to understand the precise state of affairs across all aspects of the business, including customer relations, employee morale and financial performance.

Secondly, Schultz knew that Starbucks was not just a collection of coffee shops, but a complex **system** involving supply chains, human resources, branding and customer experience. He understood the interrelationships between these elements and how changes in one could affect others. He also identified where the system was failing—in this case, in the areas of *customer experience* and *brand differentiation*.

Thirdly, Schultz understood the **processes** that underpinned Starbucks' operations—from coffee sourcing and preparation to customer service—and how these were not delivering the desired outcomes.

In response, Schultz closed all Starbucks stores in the US for several hours for a company-wide retraining, emphasising the importance of coffee-making and customer service. He also shifted the focus back to the quality of the coffee and the in-store experience, differentiating Starbucks from competitors who were trying to win over customers with cheaper prices.

This renewed focus on the core values and processes of Starbucks, as informed by Schultz's situation awareness, eventually led to the successful turnaround of the company.

From wicked problems to wicked opportunities

As I was drafting this chapter, I suddenly stopped and thought, 'Clive, you've done it again'. What I meant was that in framing the first principle of SORTED almost exclusively as an endlessly hazardous landscape demanding unceasing vigilance, I was giving a skewed picture of risk management.

For any number of reasons (e.g., fear of failure, limited resources, a conservative organisational culture, etc.), leaders often focus on *adverse risks*, in terms of threats to the organisation. But risk is not something that is inherently bad: there are also *positive risks* that can bring us previously untapped benefits or opportunities. In such cases, a willingness to take calculated risks can be a driver of future success, while forgoing this in the name of caution can limit the organisation's ability to innovate and grow, as well as creating a generalised culture of anxiety that can adversely affect the motivation and engagement of employees.

Above, we saw how Lego responded to a wicked problem that threatened their business with a strategic pivot that, while certainly daring, was also innately defensive. Let's now look at an example of another world-famous brand that, perceiving a *wicked opportunity*, took a positive risk by overhauling its entire business model to take advantage of it.

CASE STUDY
Netflix, 2007

In the mid-2000s, Netflix was a DVD rental-by-mail service competing with traditional video rental stores. However, as the internet became faster and more widespread, the company's leadership recognised the potential of online streaming as the future of media consumption [34].

In 2007, Netflix took the positive risk of launching a streaming service alongside its DVD rental business. This decision required significant investments in technology, content licensing and infrastructure, and also rested on a potentially precarious foundation: streaming technology was still relatively new and untested, and there was no guarantee that consumers would embrace the change.

As we know now, that gamble paid off. Netflix's streaming service rapidly gained popularity, and the company became the dominant player in the 'direct-to-consumer' industry. Additionally, the company continued to innovate by investing in its own original content on top of licensing properties from other studios, which made them a major player on the production side along with their status as the market leader in internet distribution.

The obsolescence of DVD as the primary home-viewing medium could have spelled disaster for Netflix. But, by staying attuned to the weak signals of the rapid advancement and adoption of streaming technology, the company transformed what could have been a wicked problem into a wicked opportunity—to such an extent that, more than a decade later, such deep-pocketed competitors as Disney, Comcast and Warner Bros. Discovery are still straining to catch up to their lead.

The case of Netflix demonstrates why, as they seek to inculcate situation awareness in both themselves and their organisation, leaders should develop a balanced approach to risk management that considers both negative and positive risks. They should also foster a culture of innovation and calculated risk-taking that encourages team members to think creatively and explore new ideas. This helps the organisation to identify and capitalise on opportunities that can lead to further growth and success.

CONCLUSION

In the first principle of SORTED, we aim to gain a *deep understanding* of both our external business environment, and the internal workings of our business model and strategic planning. We must also develop our *situation awareness*, both individually and collectively, to spot the *weak signals* of wicked problems before they arise and help us identify the wicked opportunities they could present.

In this chapter, we have examined the case of a company that spectacularly and tragically fell victim to a wicked problem in the Hickson fire, and three examples of individuals or organisations—Burry, Lego and Netflix—that perceived an impending wicked problem, and took actions with which to tame it and channel it to their advantage. In the next chapter, we will take a look at how defining our *specific goals* when seeking to tame wicked problems can increase our chances of transforming them from merely averted disasters into profitable wicked opportunities.

objective

Enron, 2001

In 2001, the once highly regarded energy company Enron collapsed due to fraudulent accounting practices and appallingly unethical business conduct. What led to such a dramatic downfall? In short, the company's corporate values, vision and mission were radically misaligned with the reality of its practices [35].

Enron's stated values were 'respect, integrity, communication and excellence'. In practice, the company's culture promoted unethical behaviour, greed and a relentless pursuit of profits, with employees encouraged to manipulate financial results and deceive investors.

The company's original vision was 'to become the premier natural-gas pipeline in America'. However, the company's focus on aggressive growth and short-term profits led it to engage in high-risk ventures in unregulated markets worldwide, often with little regard for long-term consequences.

Enron's mission was, 'we treat others as we would like to be treated ourselves. We do not tolerate abusive or disrespectful treatment. Ruthlessness, callousness, and arrogance don't belong here.' In reality, the company's fraudulent accounting practices and lack of transparency ultimately destroyed shareholder value and damaged the trust of the company's customers and employees. Indeed, its executive team regularly exercised every vice named in its mission.

The result of all this was one of the largest corporate scandals in history. The company's bankruptcy led to thousands of job losses, wiped out billions of dollars in shareholder value, and eroded public trust in the corporate world.

T HE ENRON example highlights how, in a world of wicked problems and opportunities, it is crucial for organisations to ensure that their values, vision and mission are clearly defined, consistently aligned and practised throughout the company. This is the subject that we will discuss in this chapter, under the umbrella of SORTED Principle II—*Objective*.

Once we have mapped out our *Situation* to the best of our ability, our next step is to determine the desired endpoint(s) for *after* we have addressed the wicked problem or leveraged the wicked opportunity. That determination begins from the base of our organisational *values*, *vision* and *mission*, and continues through the formulation of *authentic and purposeful objectives*—which, as we shall see, connects us back to the situation awareness we covered in our previous chapter.

Values, vision and mission

Values: What Do You Stand For?

A clear set of organisational values is essential when dealing with wicked problems [36]. They serve as a foundation for decision-making, giving us guiderails for weighing different options or trade-offs when faced with a wicked problem, and providing us with a sense of direction and purpose as we navigate these challenges. And, given that wicked problems can often involve potential ethical dilemmas, our group values can help us maintain a solid moral compass as we grapple with sometimes painful choices.

But of course, values aren't simply a safeguard against the extreme situations of wicked problems—like situation awareness, they are a crucial component of our everyday organisational existence, on both a collective and individual level. Articulating and consistently adhering to organisational values fosters collaboration and builds trust and credibility with our partners.

A solid foundation of values also supports the emotional and mental resilience of our workforce, helping individuals persevere through challenges and setbacks and stay focused on and committed to the organisation's ultimate goals and objectives. And, at their highest peak, commitment to a powerful set of values can help shape societal discourse and drive meaningful change.

The purpose statement of The Body Shop exemplifies all these aspects of organisational values, and even frames them within the context of two particularly pressing wicked problems: social and economic inequality, and climate change.

We exist to fight for a fairer, more beautiful world ... We believe in the beauty of the planet and the good in people, but our world needs work. Nature is suffering at our hands, whole species are becoming extinct in our lifetimes, and our society remains desperately, deeply unfair and unequal. Our founder, Dame Anita Roddick, built The Body Shop to fight for what is good, and just, and beautiful. Today, this fight is still at the heart of everything we do.

Even as we can be rightfully moved by this ringing rallying cry, we can also recognise how artfully the company has baked the core element of its business—ethical beauty products—into its statement of values. In so doing, The Body Shop not only issues a broad appeal to all those concerned with the state of society and the planet, but also establishes its products and services as a cornerstone of that greater cause.

Your organisational values should reflect the core purpose of your organisation, and the impact you want to have on customers, employees and society.

How do you go about formalising these into a statement of purpose such as The Body Shop's above?

- Examine the history of your organisation's culture, successes and challenges. What were the beliefs and attitudes that influenced past decisions and actions?

- Invite the feedback of key stakeholders, including founders, leaders, employees, customers and partners. Look for common themes, and use their perspectives and insights to build out a fuller picture of how your organisation operates and how its actions resonate both internally and externally.

- Narrow down this list of common themes to a manageable number—typically between three and seven—that best represent your organisation's guiding principles.

- Clearly define and articulate each of these values so that they are *unique*, *meaningful* and *actionable*.

- Communicate these formalised values to all stakeholders, and integrate them into your organisation's culture, policies and daily activities through such mechanisms as training, performance evaluations, reward systems, etc.

- Periodically review and reassess these values to ensure they remain relevant to both your organisation's purpose, and the evolving external environment. Be prepared to adjust as needed to maintain this alignment.

Vision: Where Do You Want to Be?

A clear and compelling vision clarifies your organisation's purpose, defining an overarching goal and prioritising the actions that will help realise that goal. It engages stakeholders by concisely and forcefully communicating the organisation's intentions and aims, and its innately ambitious framing can help inspire innovation and creativity within both leadership and the workforce.

Furthermore, a strong vision helps build organisational resilience to wicked problems, in a number of ways. A vision's future focus helps organisations maintain a long-term view that better enables them to seek out root causes of problems or challenges rather than focusing on symptoms—a decided advantage when faced with wicked problems.

Moreover, a strong vision aligns and motivates your employees, fostering commitment and unity, which is particularly important when facing the complex and ambiguous situations that wicked problems present.

The vision of the electric car manufacturer Tesla succinctly addresses one of the principal wicked problems of our time: carbon emissions caused by petroleum-powered vehicles.

To create the most compelling car company of the 21st century by driving the world's transition to electric vehicles.

Like The Body Shop (albeit here implicitly rather than explicitly), in its vision Tesla evokes the ideal of a better, more sustainable future to be accomplished through its product. But further, in the use of the word 'compelling', the vision statement fuses that selfless goal with the multifaceted promise of an enhancement of its customers' quality of life—which Tesla pursues through a combination of such qualities as affordability, convenience and leisure (in its attempts at self-driving vehicles), all sewn up in a seamless, 'future-cool' image.

Your organisational vision should grow organically out of your core values, as we covered in the section above. Once these are locked in, you need to build on SORTED Principle I—our old friend situation awareness—to analyse your organisation's current internal situation and the external environment in which it operates, via the following steps:

- Consider the *strengths*, *weaknesses*, *opportunities* and *threats* that may influence your organisation's future—what is known as SWOT analysis.

- Determine the fundamental *purpose* of your organisation, beyond just making a profit.

- Identify those areas where you want to make a meaningful impact on your customers, employees and society as a whole.

- Based on those impact areas, ascertain what 'success' will look like, and how your organisation's values will help shape that success.

- Finally, imagine the desired future state of your organisation, the role it will play in the world, and the legacy you want it to leave behind.

Once you have completed this process, boil it all down to a concise *vision statement* that captures the essence of your organisation's purpose and values. Make sure that it's direct, inspiring and easy to understand—your vision statement should be something that others can rally around. Then, as we did with your core values above, you should:

- Share your vision statement with a diverse range of stakeholders (including employees, customers and partners), gather their feedback, and adjust your statement to ensure that it resonates with your audience while still remaining aligned with your values.

- Embed that vision within the day-to-day processes of strategic planning, decision-making, employee training and development.

- Regularly review your vision statement to ensure that it remains relevant, resonant and aligned with your values.

Mission: What Do You Do?

Your organisational mission is how you translate your values and vision into action. It not only defines the spheres of your activity—i.e., the impact areas we covered in 'Vision', above—but also describes *how* you will create the impact you want to have. It's a 'plan of attack' that channels the solidarity and sense of purpose you generated with your values and vision into concrete, constituent *objectives*.

And, it almost goes without saying, having a clearly defined mission will equip your organisation with an enhanced resilience when tackling wicked problems. Firmly knowing *what* you're doing and *why* you're doing it will give you clarity on your situation, and enable you to better devise alternative tactics to deal with the new situation.

IDEO is a firm that provides creative solutions for businesses by merging insights, design and strategy to tackle complex challenges and transform ideas into meaningful, tangible products and services (e.g., the creation of the PillPack, a system that organises and delivers medications). Its mission statement is as follows:

IDEO is a design company known for its human-centred, interdisciplinary approach. As early leaders in the practice of design thinking, we create positive impact through design by applying our creative mindsets and skills, and by teaching others to do the same. We help clients and customers around the world build the "capacity and outcomes required to navigate today's complexity and lead their markets.

As problem solvers, we drive change, build new ventures, and design digital and tangible experiences for business, social, and governmental sectors through co-creation with our clients. As teachers, we help individuals, teams and organisations cultivate the confidence they need to step into the future with optimism and creativity.

IDEO's mission statement positions the company as not just a service provider, but a thought leader, mentor and long-term partner for their clients. By emphasising co-creation, the mission statement underscores the company's ethos of collaboration and mutual contribution, replacing the traditional, transactional consultant-client relationship with a deeper partnership. And finally, the stated goal of helping clients 'step into the future with optimism and creativity' hinges its operations to an almost utopian vision of both individual achievement and general societal progress.

To create a mission statement organically from values and vision:

- Consider how your organisation's values shape its operations. For example, if one of your values is 'innovation', how is that manifested in what your leaders and workers do on a day-to-day basis?

- Next, analyse how these actions contribute to your larger organisational vision. To continue with the previous example, how does promoting innovation help you achieve your long-term goals?

- Now, combine these insights to craft a mission statement that encapsulates what your organisation *does* (based on your values), where it aims to *go* (based on vision), and how it proposes to *get there*.

Mission possible: Setting authentic, purposeful objectives for your organisation

In business and management theory, an *objective* is a forecasted future or desired result that individuals and teams envision, plan for and commit to achieve [37]. In their foundational research on organisational psychology, Edwin Locke and Gary Latham determined that clearly defined objectives heighten both organisational and individual performance in three principal ways:

1. They *direct attention and more significant effort* towards activities related to those objectives.

2. They *increase persistence* and *prolong efforts* to achieve them.

3. They indirectly *stimulate interest*, promoting the discovery and use of strategies and knowledge relevant to the task.

Furthermore, in the goal-setting theory that Locke and Latham developed out of their research, they stress the importance of *setting the bar high* when it comes to devising organisational objectives. In this principle, Locke and Latham's theory of goal-setting goes against the grain of one of the most prominent methods for determining organisational objectives: the SMART system, which stresses the setting of goals that are *specific*, *measurable*, *achievable*, *relevant* and *time-bound*.

While the authors would surely agree with a number of those points, when it comes to the matter of achievability they recommend that organisations should select goals that are in the ninetieth percentile of difficulty—in other words, objectives that may not in fact be achievable. These are called *stretch objectives*, and the authors justify their case for them as follows [38]:

> 'Specific, difficult goals lead to higher performance than either easy goals or instructions to "do your best", as long as feedback about progress is provided, the person is committed to the goals, and the person has the ability and the knowledge to perform the task.'

In this core belief, Locke and Latham's concept of stretch objectives aligns with the thinking of Jim Collins and Jerry Porras, who appropriated an old bit of engineering vernacular—'Big Hairy A***d

Goals'—and gentrified it into the somewhat more polite 'Big Hairy Audacious Goal', or 'BHAG' [39]. As with stretch objectives, BHAGs engage people through their visceral ambition; they're aspirational, clear and compelling, demanding our commitment and promising the giddy thrill of (positive) risk.

I like the concept of BHAGs, and it is used widely and enthusiastically. However, I also think it's vital that leaders set *visible, realistic sub-goals* to support their people in feeling success along the way to the Big Hairy Audacious one. Moreover, both BHAGs and their constituent sub-goals must be determined not because they look good on paper, but by dint of the fact that they resonate with the values, vision and mission of the organisation setting them.

By adding these *authentic, purposeful objectives* to that foundation, an organisation not only sets itself up for success in a 'normal' business environment, but also equips itself with an even more potent capability to address the wicked problems that our VUCA world throws at us. Authentic, purposeful objectives provide a clear pathway to action in such scenarios, helping prevent 'paralysis by analysis'.

Even more importantly, such objectives keep the organisation anchored to its core identity and purpose while dealing with a crisis. This sustainability is key for navigating wicked problems, which require long-term commitment and cannot be solved by short-term, surface-level fixes.

An excellent example of an organisation devising authentic, purposeful goals to address wicked problems is the United Nations' strategy for sustainable development goals (SDGs), which propose strategies for taming both the climate crisis and global inequality [40].

CASE STUDY
The United Nations Sustainable Development Goals

Adopted by the UN in 2015, SDGs aim to eliminate inequality, protect the planet, and ensure universal peace and prosperity by 2030. The seventeen goals in the UN's plan cover many areas, including poverty, hunger, education, gender equality, clean water and sanitation, sustainable cities, and responsible consumption and production.

The SDGs emerged from a highly collaborative process involving a diverse range of stakeholders, including governments, the private sector, the public, academia and international non-profits. Collating the perspectives and priorities from all these different actors, the SDGs are innately interconnected—in many instances, achieving one of these goals entails making progress on multiple other goals, not as a precondition but as part of a genuinely holistic approach.

Here are three that I have adopted as goals of my charitable giving:

- **SDG 13. Climate action**—*take urgent action to combat climate change and its impacts*. Climate change is a real and undeniable threat to our entire civilisation. Through education, innovation and adherence to our climate commitments, we can make the necessary changes to protect the planet. These changes also provide huge opportunities to modernise our infrastructure, which will create new jobs and promote greater prosperity across the globe.

- **SDG 4. Quality education**—*ensure inclusive and equitable quality education and promote lifelong learning opportunities for all.* Education is key to prosperity and opens a world of opportunities, making it possible for each of us to contribute to a progressive, healthy society. Learning benefits every human being, and should be available to all.

- **SDG 3. Good health and well-being**—*ensure healthy lives and promote well-being for all at all ages.* Over the last fifteen years, the number of childhood deaths has been cut in half. This proves that it is possible to win the fight against almost every disease. Still, we are spending an astonishing amount of money and resources on treating illnesses that are surprisingly easy to prevent. The new goal for worldwide health promotes healthy lifestyles, preventive measures and modern healthcare for everyone.

Setting forward-thinking goals such as these, especially in the context of a VUCA environment, is more than just a strategic move for organisations—it's a necessity. Organisations that clearly define and pursue their objectives not only navigate the complexities of the current marketplace, but also shape the future. They become leaders, not just followers.

Delineating clear goals, akin to the spirit of the SDGs, allows organisations to direct their resources, both human and material, towards a unified vision. Such direction fosters innovation, empowers employees, and creates an environment where adaptability thrives. In today's competitive business ecosystem, complacency can be an organisation's downfall. Hence, having clear, actionable goals is akin to charting a map in an ever-shifting terrain.

Moreover, these goals, especially when they resonate with global priorities like sustainability, equity and innovation, can amplify an organisation's impact beyond its immediate stakeholders: they have the power to influence industry standards, consumer behaviour, and even public policy. By setting these kinds of objectives, organisations can not only ensure their own commercial success, but also secure a meaningful place for themselves in the rapidly evolving tapestry of tomorrow.

How Many Objectives Should You Set?

In *The 4 Disciplines of Execution,* Chris McChesney and his colleagues advocate for creating a small set of objectives to deal with the 'whirlwind' of business as usual [41]—an approach that, as we will see later in this chapter, is also optimal for dealing with the comparable hurricane of a wicked problem. In the view of McChesney et al:

> 'Your chances of achieving two or three goals with excellence are high, but the more goals you try to juggle at once, the less likely you will be to reach them.'

Why should this be so?

Allowing for some reasoned debate in the scientific community, the consensus view is that the human brain cannot perform two tasks requiring high-level brain functions simultaneously. George Miller's research into the psychology of learning found that most adults can only store five to nine elements in their short-term memory [42]. From this, Miller theorised that human memory has only a certain number of 'slots' for storing information; and, rather than expanding that capacity as we gather more info, we simply 'chunk' what additional material we can into those predetermined slots.

This limitation is intrinsically related to our brain physiology. The prefrontal cortex, the brain's main 'doorway', is designed for only a small number of inputs. Multi-tasking not only goes directly against that inherent limitation, but also weakens and erodes its advantages—namely, our brain's ability to engage with a single input deeply, attentively and creatively [43].

Some people in highly demanding professions, such as the fighter pilots we discussed in the previous chapter, may appear to have mastered the skill of multi-tasking. But remember the mantra of Tom Cruise's Maverick in the first *Top Gun*: 'If you think up there, you're dead.' Rather than multi-tasking, highly functional individuals like pilots *mimic* multi-tasking through their ability to rapidly switch from task to task—and even this is only accomplishable through years of intense training.

This is why so many countries have made it illegal for anyone (pilots included, never mind the vast majority of us who don't have the benefit of such training) to drive a car and use a mobile phone in one's hand at the same time—because it's a fundamental cognitive challenge that could have life-or-death stakes. And this same inability extends to business objectives as well, which is why even the most brilliant minds in business focus on only a handful of objectives—what McChesney and his colleagues refer to as 'wildly important' products, goals or ideas.

Combining the work of Miller and McChesney et al with my experiences mentoring leaders in various strategic projects, as well as strategic plans I've written, suggests that seven objectives plus or minus two is indeed 'magical'. In other words, for me, the ideal number of objectives an organisation should set itself in ordinary circumstances lies somewhere between five and nine.

For example, Amazon, which was originally an online bookstore, has evolved into a global e-commerce and technology titan by adhering to a few key strategic objectives. Central to their mission is an unwavering focus on customer-centricity, driving them to innovate based on user needs. This ethos enabled revolutionary offerings like Amazon Prime's rapid shipping. Their pursuit of operational efficiency, global expansion and continuous diversification has led them to dominate in cloud computing with Amazon Web Services (AWS), venture into physical retail via Whole Foods, and even explore space through Blue Origin. Moreover, with their Climate Pledge, they underscore a commitment to sustainability, targeting net-zero carbon by 2040. These strategies showcase Amazon's adaptability and ambition, which has helped them cement their market leadership.

Tackling Wicked Problems with Authentic and Purposeful Objectives

If our everyday work demands that we focus only on the most important and pressing issues, the same goes double for wicked problems, which add a whole other degree of difficulty. The multifaceted, multicausal nature of wicked problems can conjure up a whole range of potential objectives, but trying to tackle too many of these at once leads to confusion, lack of focus and a dilution of resources. Focusing on only a few prioritised objectives within the context of a wicked problem:

- simplifies the complex or chaotic situation by breaking it down into manageable pieces;

- allows teams to channel their energy and resources towards these designated target areas, rather than spreading them thinly across several;

- facilitates clearer communication and collaboration between teams and team members;

- maintains momentum and motivation to deal with the crisis; and

- makes measuring progress easier, and gives clearer indication of when strategies need to be adjusted.

How, then, do we determine our authentic, purposeful (and limited) objectives when dealing with a wicked problem? In short, we:

i   Define the problem

ii Identify our ideal outcome(s)

iii Prioritise the objectives that will realise those outcomes

Let's look at each one of these steps in turn, accompanied by case studies of organisations that performed them effectively when dealing with the same, particularly pressing wicked problem: sustainability.

i. Define the problem

1 Identify the problem—gather stakeholder information, review data and reports, conduct research, etc.

2 Seek a *deep understanding* of the problem—break it into smaller parts, analyse from different perspectives, etc.

3 Through this analysis, locate the *root cause(s)* of the problem, and define it specifically and concisely so as to allow the formulation of specific, concise objectives.

CASE STUDY
Patagonia Inc.

With its novel line of climbing equipment that wouldn't harm mountains and eco-conscious textiles, the 1972 catalogue of Chouinard Equipment—the precursor to the outdoor clothing and gear company Patagonia—already evinced the dedication to ecological sustainability and ethical product creation that would define the brand over the ensuing decades. In 1986, after officially recognising the fashion industry it belonged to as one of the major contributors to global pollution and environmental degradation [44], the company pledged to donate either 1% of its total sales or 10% of its total profits each year to environmental non-profits and advocacy groups. This commitment has been upheld annually for nearly four decades, resulting in contributions exceeding $100 million.

That first move in the late 1980s was further justified when, in 1991, Patagonia commissioned an internal life cycle assessment to assess the environmental impact of its raw materials. The study's findings were striking: despite its natural origins, the cotton the company used was far from environmentally friendly. Traditional cotton farming involved intensive water use and heavy pesticide application, which contributed to soil degradation, water contamination and harm to wildlife.

This realisation prompted Patagonia to transition to organically grown cotton in 1996, despite the challenges and higher costs involved. From this point forward, Patagonia continued to scrutinise every aspect of its supply chain, identifying areas where its operations could be made more sustainable and less harmful to the environment.

By thus defining not only the overarching wicked problem of environmental degradation, but also the ways in which its own operations were continuing to contribute to it, Patagonia was able to start formulating an array of objectives that would allow it to address these problems. These go beyond the core areas of life cycle assessment and supply chain transparency to the company's dedicated support for educational campaigns, grassroots movements, and other third-party initiatives designed to promote sustainability and environmental preservation.

ii. Identify desired outcomes

1 At the risk of sounding like a broken record on this subject (I certainly don't want you snoozing!), *engage key stakeholders* such as employees, customers and partners—all of whom are essential parts of your situation awareness system—and consider their perspectives regarding the desired outcomes of your solution to the problem.

2 Ensure that the desired outcomes *align with the organisation's mission, vision and values*—even if aspects of the business need to change in order to successfully deal with the wicked problem, you should never totally overturn your organisational essence.

3 *Measure progress* towards those desired outcomes by developing metrics or key performance indicators (KPIs).

CASE STUDY
Unilever

As did Patagonia, in 2010 the global consumer goods company Unilever recognised the wicked problem of sustainability, and how its business was contributing to that crisis [45]. As a result, the company developed a comprehensive Sustainable Living Plan that comprised three ambitious goals, which were tied to the UN Sustainable Development Goals stretching across its value chain:

- By 2020, helping more than a billion people take action to improve their health care.

- By 2030, halving the environmental footprint of the making and use of their products as they grow their business.

- By 2020, enhancing the livelihoods of millions of people as they grow their business.

The Sustainable Living Plan was fully aligned to Unilever's values, vision and mission, and while it did fall short on some of its desired outcomes (which the company was up front about), Unilever's performance against its goals was impressive. The plan's successor, the Unilever Compass Strategy, is even more strongly linked to 'superior performance', as well as 'sustainable and responsible growth' [46]. The company's current stated purpose is to 'make sustainable living commonplace', an aim that is formulated from a matrix of clear-eyed strategic realisations—'companies with purpose last', 'people with purpose thrive', and 'brands with purpose grow'—and aligned with otherwise conventional strategic goals (e.g., a growth product portfolio, leading brands, growth markets, 'channel' leadership) and specific action plans.

Values, vision, mission and objectives are even more tightly interwoven in addressing eight wicked problems identified by the UN. It is a model for how a highly conventional business can embrace taming wicked problems, placing them at the heart of strategy.

iii. Prioritise objectives

1   Identify which desired outcomes will not only provide the short-term benefit of helping to tame the wicked problem, but also help further the organisation's progress towards the long-term goals that are necessary for its sustained success.

2   Assess the feasibility of each objective, in terms of resources, timeframe, etc.

3   Rank your objectives in importance based on the best-possible balance between steps one and two, and be prepared to rearrange those rankings based on changing circumstances or new information.

CASE STUDY
Kroger

Recognising a key wicked problem for the food and beverage industry—reducing food waste to contribute to sustainability while simultaneously safeguarding profitability—the US grocery chain Kroger formulated and prioritised four key objectives to achieve its goal of reducing its food waste by 50% by 2025 [47]:

- Collaborate with suppliers to implement more sustainable practices, such as reducing overproduction and diverting food waste to alternative uses such as animal feed or composting.

- Implement new inventory management systems to optimise ordering and reduce food waste due to spoilage or expiration.

- Partner with local food banks and non-profits to donate surplus food.

- Launch campaigns to educate customers on reducing food waste, and incentivise them to purchase items nearing their expiration date.

By prioritising these objectives, Kroger has successfully reduced food waste by 35% since 2018, and is on track to achieve its goal of 50% by 2025. These efforts have also led to cost savings for the company, and improved its reputation as a socially responsible organisation.

CONCLUSION

In this chapter, we've examined how to combine our situation awareness with our inward-looking understanding of who we are and what we do as an organisation—our *values*, *vision* and *mission*. We have also aligned that with our recognition of the fact that there are only so many goals we can properly focus on and pursue at once, meaning that the objectives we do set have to be *authentic* to our character as an organisation, and *purposeful* in defining those areas where we want to make a true impact in the world.

Finally, we studied how we can then take these foundational methods of self-knowledge and purpose, and apply them to wicked problems. Because remember, even though wicked problems can represent a sometimes drastic challenge to the reality we take for granted, their causes are entirely rooted in that same reality—which means that the most important tools we've developed for shaping reality still have power, even in the most extreme situations.

At the same time, however, we have to recognise just how far those tools can take us when it comes to dealing with wicked problems, and whether some of them may actually be exacerbating the problem. Being able to examine ourselves and our operations *critically* is essential in such scenarios, and it constitutes the crux of the next principle in the SORTED model.

reality

Bristol Royal Infirmary Inquiry, 1992-98

Beginning in 1984, a number of investigations were launched into practices in the paediatric cardiac surgery ward at the Bristol Royal Infirmary (BRI), after medical professionals started raising concerns about the high mortality rates among the young patients [48, 49]. These concerns were primarily related to two surgeons, James Wisheart and Janardan Dhasmana.

In 1992, an internal review identified higher-than-average mortality rates for specific heart surgeries performed on children, but the study did not lead to significant changes in hospital practice. In response, some parents of patients in the ward began to form support groups to share their experiences, and also put pressure on outside bodies to give greater scrutiny to the BRI's paediatric cardiac surgery unit.

In 1995, an external review by the Royal College of Surgeons found that the BRI unit's mortality rates were significantly higher than the national average, and recommended the suspension of certain complex surgeries. The report received widespread media attention, prompting a public outcry and further investigations. In 1997 and '98, the General Medical Council (GMC) conducted disciplinary hearings with Wisheart and Dhasmana, and ultimately found them guilty of serious professional misconduct. Wisheart was struck off the medical register, while Dhasmana was suspended from practising for three years.

Following the GMC's verdict, the UK government announced that the BRI would be the object of a public inquiry, with the goal of making recommendations for improving the overall safety and quality of paediatric cardiac surgery in the UK. I contributed to the inquiry, addressing a workshop focused on organisational learning which aimed to contextualise the individual failings of the two surgeons within the framework of an organisational/systemic failure that allowed them to perpetuate their sometimes fatal errors.

As the assorted investigations revealed, Wisheart and Dhasmana had exhibited an almost systematic refusal of critical thinking in their conduct, including but not limited to:

- continuing to perform complex paediatric cardiac surgeries despite concerns from colleagues and other medical professionals about high mortality rates in the unit and potential issues with the quality of care;

- displaying an overconfidence in their abilities that potentially contributed to their failure to acknowledge the severity of the problem, and prevented them seeking assistance, additional training or collaboration with other experts;

- appearing resistant to change, despite evidence suggesting that their established procedures were not meeting national standards of care;

- failing to establish a culture of transparency and accountability by not adequately communicating with colleagues, hospital management and patients' families; and,

- through this failure, contributing to a breakdown in trust and creating an environment that hindered other staff from effectively addressing the problem.

T HE INQUIRY into the BRI concluded in 2001, and produced recommendations that led to significant reforms to the UK's National Health Service (NHS) in the areas of patient safety, clinical governance and transparency. While this is laudable, it is also tragic that a systemic lack of critical thinking about the *reality* of the situation at BRI created and perpetuated a wicked problem that caused injury to so many. This is the subject we tackle in SORTED Principle III—honing your ability to look critically at your precepts, prejudices and blind spots, and overcoming the socio-psychological barriers to critical thinking.

What's the point of critical thinking?

The innate complexity or chaos of wicked problems often makes it difficult for individuals and organisations to thoroughly grasp the reality of these situations. Sometimes, people oversimplify or overlook essential aspects of the problem, leading to misguided or ineffective solutions. Alternatively, the sheer magnitude of volatility, uncertainty, ambiguity, turbulence and conflicting information inherent in the problem can make gathering accurate data challenging, and inspire a feeling of paralysis or inability to act effectively.

Critical thinking helps us better understand the reality of a wicked problem by systematically analysing and evaluating information so that we can devise practical solutions founded on well-reasoned judgement. It builds on the situation awareness we developed in Principle I, and the foundation of values, vision and mission we defined in Principle II, by compelling us to *question* our observations and assumptions, *challenge* our biases, and *consider multiple perspectives* so that we can better understand the underlying causes of a wicked problem.

This is all the more crucial in our current age of 'everyday' artificial intelligence. While machines can collect and present vast amounts of data, it is still down to humans to analyse and act on this information in order to keep our organisations (and society) running. For example, while accountants use AI platforms to automate mundane tasks such as preparing accounts, issuing invoices and creating balance sheets, the purpose of this automation is to allow them to focus on *interpreting* the data to provide insights to their clients. In this way, we employ artificial intelligence to better provide our human-derived, *augmented intelligence*—the bedrock of organisational success, innovation and growth, and also a primary weapon for taming wicked problems.

Even as we venture further into an automated world, the fundamental tenets of critical thinking have remained effectively unchanged since the days of the 'original critical thinker': Socrates, or rather, the Socrates that has come down to us through the *Dialogues* of Plato [50]. Socrates believed that an interrogative soul was the essential requirement of a virtuous life, and that ethics cannot be dictated by authority. Rather, true virtue must be divined by parsing evidence, scrutinising common rationales and assumptions, and, where these beliefs do not align with reality—the reality that we are able to discern through sound, systematic reasoning and logical consistency—they should be revealed as the potentially damaging fabrications that they are. And that principle still applies to our even more complex and chaotic world today, with all the multiplying wicked problems that our short-sightedness and unfounded beliefs have helped foster.

The three barriers to critical thinking

Before we discuss techniques that can help you improve your critical thinking, it's essential that we understand the barriers to that kind of self-examination in an organisational context. Three of the most prevalent socio-psychological phenomena that inhibit critical thinking are *groupthink*, *escalation of commitment* and *polythink syndrome*.

Groupthink

Groupthink was extensively researched by Irving Janis, who used the Bay of Pigs disaster and the Japanese attack on Pearl Harbor as his primary case studies [51, 52]. This model, which has influenced research on corporate and political leadership and decision-making in teams, has the following features:

- Groupthink arises within tightly knit groups ('ingroups'), which fosters a desire for uniformity that often reads silence as agreement.

- The group's cohesion is maintained by 'mind guards', who filter dissenting opinions and manipulate information flow.

- The ingroup often overestimates its abilities and undervalues the views of potential opponents of its views—defined as an 'outgroup'—leading to biases, discrimination, and an overlooking of the potential negative ramifications of their actions.

- The group tends to ignore views from the outgroup that contradict their beliefs, and associate the outgroup's cautions or qualifications with weakness or malice.

- In the face of this, members of the outgroup may feel compelled to conform to avoid creating negative impressions, which can lead to self-censorship.

This dysfunctional dynamic can arise from the interaction of multiple factors, from the situational (e.g., high stress, time pressure, recent failures) to the constitutional (e.g., a lack of clear structure, rules and decision-making processes, which can allow dominant personalities to unduly influence group decisions). Whatever particular form it takes, group-think acts as a hindrance to genuine critical thinking by fostering a culture of conformity, overconfidence and limited perspective.

Escalation of Commitment

As theorised by Barry Staw, escalation of commit-ment refers to the phenomenon whereby individuals or organisations continue to invest resources (time, money, effort) in a decision or project even when it becomes apparent that it may not be the best course of action [53–56]. This can be driven by a number of factors, including:

- **Groupthink.** As discussed above, an overwhelming desire for conformity and consensus can con-vince organisations to continue on an ill-advised path rather than entertaining dissenting or alter-native opinions.

- **Confirmation bias.** Individuals or organisations may selectively 'cherry-pick' information that supports their initial decision or investment, and ignore or downplay data that contradicts it.

- **Loss aversion.** Anxiety around the losses that would be *immediately* incurred by abandoning a failing course of action can lead actors to favour the 'death by a thousand cuts' of staying the course—even though the losses from the latter can often be far greater than the former.

- **Sunk cost fallacy.** Tied in with loss aversion, it can be difficult to cut back on a failed strategy that you have already invested plentiful resources into. The temptation to make the investment 'worth it' by seeing the (failing) plan through can override the rational choice to abandon it.

- **Self-justification.** Beyond the fear of material losses, individuals and organisations can also be sensitive to the ego-driven 'loss of face' that would occur if they were to admit their initial decision was a mistake, and to perversely double down on that error by continuing to push a failing strategy.

Escalation of commitment can counteract critical thinking in several ways. It can impair objectivity, as individuals or groups heavily invested in a decision may become emotionally attached to its outcomes, clouding their ability to make rational judgements. Further, this commitment can lead to resistance to new, potentially contradictory information, stifling open discussion and the exploration of alternatives, essential components of effective critical thinking. This resistance can further skew risk assessment.

Individuals caught in an escalation of commitment can overlook looming losses and overestimate the potential for success, despite clear indicators pointing towards the contrary.

Polythink Syndrome

As outlined by Alex Mintz and Carly Wayne [57], polythink is at the opposite end of the spectrum from the monocular biases of groupthink and escalation of commitment. Here, group members simultaneously hold and advocate for multiple, often conflicting perspectives and courses of action. While this may seem as if it promotes diverse viewpoints and stimulates debate, it can also hinder critical thinking through:

- **Information overload.** When faced with too many conflicting perspectives, group members can struggle to process and evaluate the most relevant data points and courses of action, impairing their ability to make well-informed decisions.

- **Paralysis by analysis.** Related to the above, an insistence on exhaustively considering and weighing the respective value of multiple conflicting viewpoints can make it challenging for group members to reach a consensus, and hinder the taking of timely action.

- **Conflicting loyalties.** Group members can develop strong attachments to their own perspectives and become more concerned about defending them than objectively evaluating the merits of alternative views, creating an unhealthy, competitive environment.

- **Incoherent decision-making.** If a decision *is* reached in a polythink situation, it can be little more than a patchwork of compromises between fundamentally conflicting perspectives, which will almost certainly fail to address the issue effectively.

While diversity of thought is often beneficial, polythink can impede critical thinking by causing discussion fragmentation, promoting inconsistent decisions, enhancing group polarisation, leading to insufficient evaluation of solutions, and creating information-processing issues. Consequently, it may result in decision-making that is based more on individual biases and viewpoints rather than a collective, critically evaluated consensus.

Overcoming barriers to critical thinking

Now that we know the enemies of critical thinking, how do we overcome them?

To combat groupthink, some of the general precepts to keep in mind are:

- Encourage groups to engage in healthy debate.

- Encourage diversity of thought.

- Encourage group members to speak up and voice their opinions, even if they differ from the group consensus.

- Encourage the group to consider alternative viewpoints and seek out feedback from outside the group.

Let's look at a real-life example of putting the boots to groupthink.

CASE STUDY
Apple Inc.

Apple had experienced some challenging times by the mid-'90s. After Steve Jobs was ousted in 1985, the company had gone through various CEOs and slipped into a pattern of groupthink that was stifling innovation. The management team was making seemingly 'safe' decisions to try to keep the company afloat, which resulted in many products that did not perform well in the market. They were focused on maintaining the status quo rather than pushing the boundaries of technology and design, which was their initial success point.

When Jobs returned to the company in 1997, he took significant steps to undo this pervasive groupthink mentality. He reduced the number of projects and products Apple was working on, focusing instead on a few key areas where the company could truly innovate. This led to the development and launch of revolutionary products like the iPod in 2001, the iPhone in 2007, and the iPad in 2010.

Jobs also introduced a culture of challenging ideas and encouraging different perspectives in order to foster a diversity of opinion, which created space for truly innovative ideas to gain traction. Famously, he declared that, 'We don't hire smart people to tell them what to do. We hire smart people so they can tell us what to do.'

What about our next bugbear, escalation of commitment?

- Encourage stakeholders to re-evaluate their assumptions and consider alternative courses of action.

- Encourage them to weigh the costs and benefits of continuing the project versus cutting their losses and moving on.

- Encourage the development of a culture of transparency, open communication and regular reviews.

CASE STUDY
Ford Motor Company

Sedans were among the most popular types of vehicle in the mid-20th century, and, like other automobile manufacturers, Ford invested heavily in their production. As time went on, though, customer preferences began to change, and by the early 21st century many consumers were favouring trucks, SUVs and electric vehicles. Yet despite these market changes, Ford continued to stay committed to sedan production, partially due to the fact that the company had invested so much in this area that it was difficult to imagine washing their hands of it, even as the sales numbers made clear that sedans were no longer as popular or profitable as they once were.

In 2018, however, Ford made a radical decision to discontinue all of its sedan models in North America (excluding the Mustang and the Ford Focus Active) and pivot towards the increasingly popular vehicle types noted above. It was not an easy decision, considering the decades-long investment and the jobs tied to these models' production. However, Ford had finally recognised the necessity of this strategic shift in order to meet changing customer preferences and market demands.

In the years since, Ford has seen success with models like the F-150, the Mustang Mach-E electric vehicle, and their SUV lineup, demonstrating the wisdom of their decision to overcome their previous commitment and adapt to the evolving market.

Finally, what can we bring to bear to defuse poly-think syndrome?

- Ensure that the overall objectives of the project or task are clear to all. This can serve as a common ground when reconciling diverse perspectives.

- Encourage participants to employ frameworks that allow for diverse opinions, such as the Delphi method or nominal group technique, but which allow the development of consensus.

- Encourage them to attend regular meetings where different subgroups or team members come together to discuss and integrate their distinct viewpoints, preferably with a facilitator to moderate discussion.

CASE STUDY
Spotify

Spotify adeptly counters the challenges posed by polythink using a variant of the popular Agile project management method [58]. Spotify employs a unique organisational structure with autonomous 'squads' to encourage independent decision-making, but keeps them aligned through successively larger groups (tribes, chapters and guilds). This balance between decentralisation and overarching company goals ensures diverse viewpoints converge cohesively.

Tools for immediate internal feedback quickly address conflicting perspectives. While 'Hack Days' stimulate innovation, only ideas aligning with Spotify's core values progress, ensuring the multitude of ideas doesn't divert the company's focused trajectory.

Learning to think critically

Up to this point, we've devoted most of our time to exploring the obstacles and hindrances to critical thinking. So it's about time that we started looking at how we can actually develop and refine this crucial habit, on both an individual and organisational level.

- Be open to new ideas and experiences and develop a habit of asking questions. Cultivating a curious mindset helps you learn more about different subjects and perspectives, encouraging you to think critically about the information you encounter.

- Before making any decision or forming an opinion, gather as much information as possible from various sources. Seek out diverse viewpoints and try to understand the reasoning behind different perspectives. Collecting information this way provides a solid foundation for critical thinking.

- Once you have gathered information, carefully evaluate the quality and credibility of the evidence. Consider the source, any potential biases and the methodology used to collect the data. Evaluating the evidence helps you determine the reliability of the information and make informed judgements.

- Identify the underlying assumptions in any argument or perspective and consider whether these assumptions are valid. Be aware of your assumptions and biases, and be open to questioning and re-evaluating them.

- Examine the logic and structure of the arguments presented to you. Identify any logical fallacies, inconsistencies or flaws in reasoning. Analysing the logic helps you develop a deeper understanding of the issue and make well-reasoned judgements.

- Try to put yourself in the shoes of others and understand their viewpoints, motivations and feelings. Developing empathic skills will help you better understand the issue and consider alternative perspectives.

- Weigh the evidence, consider different perspectives, and use logical reasoning to make decisions. Be prepared to change your mind if new information or better arguments emerge.

- Regularly evaluate your critical-thinking skills and be open to feedback from others. Reflect on your thoughts, the information you rely on and your decisions. Reflecting on your thinking helps you identify areas for improvement and develop stronger critical-thinking skills over time.

- Use critical-thinking skills in everyday life, whether making decisions at work, evaluating news articles, or engaging in discussions with friends and family. The more you practice, the better you will become at thinking critically.

- Critical thinking is an ongoing process that requires continuous learning and improvement. Stay informed about current events, read widely, and engage in activities that challenge your thinking, such as attending workshops, participating in debates or joining discussion groups.

To see these principles in action, let's consider the case of a world-leading company that has embedded critical thinking at the core of its operations.

CASE STUDY
Pixar

The computer animation studio Pixar owes much of its success to its unique approach to the creative process, known as the 'Braintrust' system. [59].

The Braintrust originated with the foundational group of Pixar creatives—including John Lasseter, Andrew Stanton, Pete Docter and Joe Ranft—that worked on *Toy Story*, the studio's first feature film. This group developed a rapport where they could freely critique each other's work, which they found improved the quality of their storytelling.

According the Pixar co-founder and president, Ed Catmull, the now-institutionalised form of the Braintrust evolved out of a desire to create an environment where everyone feels free to comment and criticise, without fear of retaliation or judgement [60]. This is a key tenet of critical thinking: the ability to question and challenge prevailing norms and assumptions, and to explore new ideas and perspectives.

The Braintrust convenes every few months to review each movie in production at Pixar. The meetings are not merely progress reports, but are designed for intensive problem-solving. The Braintrust watches the latest cut of a movie or individual scenes, and then provides candid and constructive feedback. The key to this process is that the feedback, while honest and often tough, is not prescriptive—the Braintrust does not tell the director how to fix things, only what isn't working.

Another aspect of Pixar's critical-thinking culture is its commitment to continuous learning and improvement. The company operates Pixar University, an in-house training centre where employees at all levels can take courses in everything from drawing and sculpture to improvisation and filmmaking. The idea is not just to improve technical skills, but also to foster a culture of curiosity, lifelong learning and intellectual exploration.

These efforts have paid off. Pixar's movies have been both critically acclaimed and commercially successful, which is a testament to the power of critical thinking in driving organisational performance. The ability to critically assess each movie during its development process allows Pixar to continually refine and improve their work, leading to better outcomes and higher performance.

CONCLUSION

There are all kinds of reasons to ignore, deny or obscure the reality before our eyes. But, as we've seen from the examples and case studies above, the quality that unites all of them is fear—whether of material losses, exclusion from the group, damage to our ego, or any number of other dread-inducing possibilities. Our situation awareness can alert us to the reality of an impending wicked problem, but without the ability to think critically and dispassionately about it—about how we can realistically tame it, what we can realistically achieve in terms of our desired outcome, and the real costs we may have to incur to accomplish the least damaging result—we can succumb to the fear not only of the extreme situation itself, but also the host of everyday fears that such situations enhance.

The good news, though, is that critical thinking can do work for us in advance of a wicked problem. By clearly and rationally assessing the range of possible threats to our organisation, we can develop plans for dealing with them should they arise—which, though they will almost certainly not offer a perfect solution in the actual event, will give us a base from which to consider our next courses of action. This is what we will explore in the next chapter.

PRINCIPLE IV

templating

Ladbroke train disaster, 1999

On 5 October, 1999, a high-speed passenger train and a local commuter train collided at Ladbroke Grove near Paddington Station in West London, due to signal failure and human error. The crash resulted in thirty-one deaths and over 520 injuries, making it one of the worst rail disasters in modern British history [61, 62].

I made a small contribution to the public inquiry that followed the accident, advising on how poor risk management contributed to the disaster. In my research on the case, I became familiar with how emergency responders employed a variety of templated solutions—in the form of established protocols, procedures and plans—to coordinate their efforts, allocate resources and communicate effectively as they sought to tame this wicked problem. These included:

- **Rapid response capabilities.** Once the incident was reported, pre-existing procedures allowed for the rapid mobilisation of emergency services, enabling them to rescue survivors and stabilise the injured as soon as possible.

- **Triage protocols.** Using established guidelines, medical teams were able to prioritise treatment of survivors based on the severity of their injuries, ensuring that the most critically injured individuals received timely care.

- **Multi-agency coordination.** The establishment of an Incident Command System (ICS) allowed for clear communication and allocation of roles and responsibilities between the emergency services from various organisations, such as the London Fire Brigade, London Ambulance Service and British Transport Police, enabling effective collaboration between these different agencies.

While it is difficult to quantify the number of lives that were saved by these measures, it is beyond doubt that the coordinated efforts of emergency services played a crucial role in minimising further casualties.

THE LADBROKE GROVE disaster and other mass casualty events like it provide the starkest examples of the reality of taming a particularly wicked problem, where the desired outcome is simply to minimise damage as much as possible. But even as it is hard to think of such situations in terms of 'success', we can still see how crucial it is for organisations to have built-in templates that not only allow them to quickly respond to wicked problems, but are also flexible enough to enable tactical decision-making as the devilish particularities of those problems present themselves.

In this chapter, we will explore how and when to create templates for wicked problems, using the 'checklist' tool and the concept of 'crisis families'. Then, we will examine how the decision-making templates we can devise from these frameworks can be applied to the organisational systems we explored in the chapter on Principle I—our *Business Model Canvas* (internal) and customer *Empathy Map* (external)—in order to give us preliminary firewalls against wicked problems.

Setting your checklist

In his book *The Checklist Manifesto: How to Get Things Right*, Atul Gawande argues that the ever-increasing complexity of tasks across so many fields often exceeds the ability of individuals—even experienced professionals—to manage them effectively, leading to errors, failures and, sometimes, catastrophes [63]. To mitigate this complexity, he suggests employing one of the most basic, but effective tools for every-day organisation ever devised: the checklist, which breaks complex tasks down into a series of simple steps. Gawande draws on examples and evidence from a number of fields in which checklists are an established tool for reducing errors and improving safety, such as aviation—where pilots use pre-flight checklists to check the integrity of critical systems and procedures before take-off and landing—or the World Health Organization (WHO), whose surgical safety checklist he helped create.

Discussing the practical aspects of creating and implementing checklists in an organisational environment, Gawande stresses three key points:

- **Simplicity**—your checklist should be easy to understand and use

- **Customisation**—your checklist should be tailored to the tasks, regulations and restrictions of your specific environment

• **Collaboration**—checklists are most effective when used within a culture that prizes teamwork and communication

How can a templated checklist be used in the taming of wicked problems, which shatter templates by definition? Precisely because they help break down that problem into manageable tasks, enabling improved communication and reducing the risk of overlooking essential steps [64]. To give you a general example of how such templating can work, see the five-stage crisis management checklist below:

1   First, a *crisis identification and assessment checklist* helps define the nature of the crisis and evaluate its potential impact on the organisation. Designated tasks may include:

a   Identifying the nature and scope of the crisis.

b   Assessing potential risks and consequences to the organisation.

c   Determining the level of urgency and prioritising response actions.

d   Identifying key stakeholders affected by the crisis.

2   Next, a *crisis response team formation checklist* provides protocols for assembling an effective crisis management team. Designated tasks may include:

a   Appointing a crisis manager or team leader.

b   Selecting team members with relevant skills and expertise.

c   Assigning roles and responsibilities to each team member.

d   Establishing communication channels and protocols for the team.

3   A *crisis communication checklist* helps guide the development and dissemination of relevant information during the crisis. Designated tasks may include:

a   Creating a communication plan, including target audiences, key messages and channels.

b   Designating spokesperson(s) for the organisation.

c   Providing regular updates to internal and external stakeholders.

d   Monitoring media coverage and public sentiment for potential issues or misinformation.

4   A *crisis mitigation and management checklist* guides the implementation of actions to address the crisis and minimise its impact on the organisation. Designated tasks may include:

a   Developing and executing a detailed action plan, including short-term and long-term measures.

b   Monitoring progress and adjusting the plan as needed.

c   Coordinating with relevant internal departments and external partners.

d   Ensuring compliance with applicable laws, regulations and industry best practices.

5   Finally, a *recovery and learning checklist* seeks to measure the effectiveness of the response and recommend actions to better safeguard the organisation in the future. Designated tasks may include:

a   Assessing the effectiveness of the crisis management efforts.

b   Identifying lessons learned and areas for improvement.

c   Implementing changes to processes, policies or procedures based on the lessons learned.

d   Conducting training and awareness sessions to improve organisational preparedness for future crises.

Now, let me note here that while creating a check-list can be a valuable tool in preparing for crisis situations, it is most effective when used as part of a broader *crisis management strategy* that is founded on three central pillars: *hazard identification* and *risk assessment*; *risk mitigation*; and *communication*. In the section below, we will examine each of these pillars in turn; then, we will illustrate how each of them can be applied to wicked problems within the five broad 'crisis families' that organisations typically face.

The three pillars of crisis management

1. Hazard Identification and Risk Assessment

Hazard identification means, precisely, detecting potential threats to the organisation through the individual and organisational situation awareness we discussed so thoroughly in our chapter on Principle I. It entails *noticing* a situation that's developing, *understanding* what that situation means in regards to the organisation, and *predicting* what could happen next if that situation is allowed to develop unchecked.

Once the hazard has been identified, it's time for risk assessment to come into play. In my own work in this field, I gauge risk along two axes:

- **Likelihood of occurrence,** on a five-point scale (Very Unlikely, Unlikely, Possible, Likely, Very Likely)

- **Impact of the hazard eventuating,** on a five-point scale (Negligible, Minor, Moderate, Major, Catastrophic)

After measuring the potential hazard on these scales, I combine the two elements in a *risk assessment matrix* (Figure 5), which visualises the results and allows us to express them numerically.

	IMPACT				
	NEGLIGIBLE (1)	MINOR (2)	MODERATE (3)	MAJOR (4)	CATASTROPHIC (5)
VERY LIKELY (5)	LOW (5)	MEDIUM (10)	MEDIUM (15)	HIGH (20)	HIGH (25)
LIKELY (4)	LOW (4)	LOW (8)	MEDIUM (12)	MEDIUM (16)	HIGH (20)
POSSIBLE (3)	LOW (3)	LOW (6)	MEDIUM (9)	MEDIUM (12)	MEDIUM (15)
UNLIKELY (2)	LOW (2)	LOW (4)	LOW (6)	MEDIUM (8)	MEDIUM (10)
VERY UNLIKELY (1)	LOW (1)	LOW (2)	LOW (3)	MEDIUM (4)	MEDIUM (5)

(LIKELIHOOD — vertical axis label)

FIGURE 5 Risk assessment matrix

The numbers in the cells of the table are calculated by multiplying the likelihood score (the row) by the impact score (the column). For example, a hazard that's 'Possible' (3) and has 'Moderate' impact (3) would have an overall risk score of 9.

To then determine the relative level of risk, you set ranges based on the maximum score possible (in this case, 25). An example could be:

- Low risk: 1-8
- Medium risk: 9-16
- High risk: 17-25

This would mean that any hazards with a score of 17 or above are considered high risk (sometimes referred to as 'showstoppers') and need immediate attention. Those with a score of 9-16 are medium risk and require management attention, while those with a score of 1-8 are low risk and can be managed with routine procedures.

However, despite all those official-looking numbers above, I want to remind you here of that key point about risk assessment that we covered in the prelude of this book: *all risk is subjective.* This means that the risk matrix is by no means a scientific tool, but a useful barometer for how an organisation's subjective appetite for risk applies to a specific, potentially hazardous situation, and it should be employed accordingly. (When I undertake a formal risk assessment with clients, I use words rather than numbers.)

2. Risk Mitigation
There are five fundamental risk mitigation actions (or 'risk controls') that can help reduce both the likelihood and impact of a hazard.

i   **Avoidance**—changing plans or processes to stave off any chance of a specific hazard eventuating

ii **Reduction**—adding safety measures, providing training, improving processes or maintaining equipment to lessen the likelihood and/or impact of a potential hazard

iii **Transference**—shifting a potentially hazardous process or activity to another party (e.g., outsourcing to a company that can manage that particular risk better), and/or offsetting the damages of that potential hazard through insurance

iv **Acceptance**—willing undertaking of certain risks according to the organisation's risk appetite (or if the cost of mitigating them is higher than the potential harm), coupled with a diligent monitoring of them to ensure that they remain within the bands of organisational tolerance

v   **Sharing**—distributing the potential impact of risk across multiple parties that share the responsibility for a certain process or activity, through partnerships, joint ventures or other forms of collaboration

3. Communication

Communication ensures that all relevant parties are informed about risks and the actions being taken to manage them. The risk management communication process typically involves the following steps:

- Identify who needs to be involved in the risk management process (e.g., employees, managers, executives, shareholders, customers) and determine their respective information needs and communication preferences.

- Devise a communication plan that outlines what information will be communicated, how often communication will occur, what methods will be used (e.g., email updates, meetings, reports), and who is responsible for conveying which types of information.

- Communicate the nature, likelihood and impact of potential risks to all relevant stakeholders once these hazards have been identified and assessed.

- If a hazard eventuates, communicate to these same stakeholders the plans that are being enacted to manage the risk—e.g., what actions are being taken, why they are being taken, and what the stakeholders' role is in implementing them.

- As risk management is an ongoing process, provide regular updates about new risks, changes to existing risks, and the effectiveness of risk management plans.

- As communication should be two-way, provide stakeholders the opportunity to ask questions, provide feedback, and contribute their own observations and suggestions to both risk assessment procedures and risk management strategies.

• Document all risk-related communications and incorporate their learnings into future risk management efforts, to help build an organisational culture that is responsive and resilient to risk.

The five 'crisis families'

As we've explored throughout this book, wicked problems are often unpredictable, can take many forms, and can shift forms with sometimes startling speed. This necessitates that, beyond your templated checklist, you have to understand which types of crises your organisation is most likely to encounter, what their impact is, and how you should respond.

In their book *Crisis Management: A Diagnostic Guide for Improving Your Organisation's Crisis-Preparedness* [65], Ian Mitroff and Christine Pearson break down crises into five groupings based on their underlying causes and characteristics. These *crisis families* can help organisations identify the nature of potential or existing crises, evaluate their vulnerabilities and improve their preparedness.

Below, we will look at each crisis family in turn, first giving an example of each crisis type, and then seeing how the pillars of risk assessment, risk mitigation and communication can be applied to them, via further real-world examples.

1   Economic Crisis

CASE STUDY
Lehman Brothers, 2008

The global financial crisis of 2007–08, triggered by a down-turn in the US housing market, had severe repercussions for many businesses, most notably Lehman Brothers. The bank's substantial investments in mortgage-backed securities depreciated rapidly as homeowners defaulted on mortgages. This devaluation led to a liquidity crisis, with other institutions wary of Lehman's stability. Despite attempts to secure a rescue deal, Lehman Brothers declared bankruptcy on 15 September 2008, marking the largest such filing in US history up to that time and intensifying the global financial turmoil.

Risk assessment: What are financial or economic events that might adversely impact your organisation's financial health and stability, and how likely are they to occur? (e.g., recession or economic downturn; sudden changes in market demand; fluctuations in exchange or interest rates; financial mismanagement or fraud)

Risk mitigation:

a **Financial controls.** Implement robust financial management, including budgeting, forecasting, auditing and fraud detection mechanisms (e.g., casinos in Australia are required to have in place strict controls to identify, mitigate and manage the risk of their products or services being misused for money laundering or terrorism financing).

b **Diversification and contingency planning.** Diversify revenue streams, maintain cash reserves, and create contingency plans for potential financial disruptions (e.g., under the Basel III international regulatory framework, banks are required to maintain capital that is at least 8% of their risk-weighted assets).

Communication: Inform stakeholders about the organisation's financial health and steps being taken to mitigate economic risks.

2. Information Crisis

CASE STUDY
Medibank hack, 2022

In October 2022, a hacker 'relieved' Australian healthcare insurer Medibank of the personal details of 9.7 million customers [66]. Later analysis revealed that, among other issues, Medibank failed to properly assess the risk of third-party access. Accordingly, relatively simple mitigation measures (e.g., the correct configuration and review of remote access) were not in place. Medibank's communications failed spectacularly in the wake of the breach. Put bluntly, it initially didn't want to inform either its customers or the media about the hack, and when it ultimately did, its messaging was spectacularly poor. For example, Medibank CEO David Koczkar said at one point that the health insurer had no idea its customers' data was sitting in the hands of criminals until it was contacted to pay a ransom—which might be brutally honest, but does not inspire confidence that the business is bringing the matter under control.

Risk assessment: What sorts of mismanagement or misuse of information might lead to adverse consequences for the organisation? (e.g., data breaches or leaks of sensitive information, misinformation or disinformation campaigns, loss or corruption of critical data, system failures, cyberattacks)

Risk mitigation:

a **Information security.** Implement information security measures, including access controls, encryption and intrusion detection systems (e.g., when GitHub was hit by a massive distributed denial of service [DDoS] attack in 2018, the company was able to mitigate the attack in less than ten minutes thanks to its robust defence mechanisms, such as proactive monitoring, and ability to switch to third-party servers [67]).

b **Data backup and recovery.** Create protocols and mechanisms to minimise data loss and ensure business continuity (e.g., all higher education institutions in Australia must demonstrate that their student data is held securely and onshore).

Communication: Develop a crisis communication plan to manage the flow of information, addressing internal and external stakeholders (e.g., GitHub provided detailed public post-mortems about the attack described above, which helped the broader online community prepare for and understand the evolving threat landscape).

3. Physical Crisis

CASE STUDY
Australian bushfires, 2019-20

The summer bushfires that ravaged Australia in 2019-20 killed thirty-three people, including six Australian firefighters and three American aerial firefighters. Thousands of homes were destroyed or damaged, and smoke blanketed much of the country, contributing to hundreds of further deaths. Nearly three billion animals were killed or displaced, and the fires harmed many threatened species and ecological communities. Overall, the fires caused billions of dollars of damage.

The subsequent Royal Commission into National Natural Disaster Arrangements [68], surfaced a number of issues with Australia's natural disaster preparedness, including inconsistencies in warnings, danger ratings and other crucial information; unnecessarily complex warnings; confusion over insurance; unclear information about land management; and more. The fact that a nation that is so used to dealing with this nearly annual physical crisis could drop the ball in so many ways illustrates how even a nominally well-prepared crisis management strategy can contain gaping holes.

Risk assessment: What are potential threats to the organisation's physical assets, such as people, property and infrastructure? (e.g., natural disasters; workplace accidents or industrial incidents; acts of terrorism or sabotage; product recalls due to safety concerns; epidemics or pandemics)

Risk mitigation:

a   **Safety and security measures.** Devise emergency preparedness plans, workplace safety protocols, facility security systems, etc. (e.g., Boeing invests heavily in safety, including rigorous testing of aircraft, intensive training programs for staff, and maintaining secure facilities to prevent espionage and theft).

b   **Contingency planning.** Locate alternative facilities, providers, etc. in the event of a major disruption to normal operations (e.g., Boeing has multiple manufacturing facilities and a diversified supplier base to ensure production isn't halted due to issues at any single location or with a specific supplier).

Communication: Create a communication plan to inform stakeholders about the organisation's response to a physical crisis, including emergency response efforts and recovery plans (e.g., in 2017, in the face of criticism and lawsuits regarding iPhone battery issues and performance slowdowns, Apple's senior leadership released a letter to its customers, explaining the technical challenges, apologising for the confusion, and offering discounted battery replacements).

4. Human Resource Crisis

CASE STUDY
'Disgusting Domino's People', 2009

In 2009, two Domino's employees in North Carolina filmed themselves performing unsanitary acts during food preparation and uploaded it to YouTube. The video quickly went viral and caused an uproar, confronting Domino's with a major public relations crisis. In response, the employees were fired and faced criminal charges. Domino's president Patrick Doyle released a video apology, emphasising that the incident wasn't representative of the brand. The company's direct response helped mitigate long-term damage, but the event underscored the challenges businesses face in the social media age. This incident is a classic example of 'brand vandalism' [69].

Risk assessment: What are potential human resource risks to the organisation, and how might they impact it? (e.g., employee misconduct or illegal activities; discrimination; harassment; hostile work environment claims; labour strikes or disputes; high employee turnover; talent shortages)

Risk mitigation:

a **Policies and procedures.** Develop and enforce clear guidelines and processes for employee conduct, workplace ethics, labour relations, etc. (e.g., in 2017, former Uber engineer Susan Fowler published a blog post detailing her experiences of sexual harassment and the company's inadequate response [70]; following the incident, Uber reviewed and overhauled its HR policies and procedures to better handle harassment claims).

b **Employee training and support.** Provide training, resources and programs designed to foster a positive workplace culture (e.g., in responding to Fowler's complaint, Uber initiated mandatory sexual harassment training for all employees and introduced new systems to report misconduct).

Communication: Implement a communication plan to address internal and external stakeholders, ensuring transparency and accountability (e.g., while the reception to his statement on the Fowler case was mixed, Uber's then-CEO Travis Kalanick publicly acknowledged the issues and promised change, and the company communicated its commitment to change, both internally and to its users).

5. Reputational Crisis

CASE STUDY
Volkswagen 'Dieselgate' scandal, 2015

In 2015, Volkswagen, one of the world's largest car manufacturers, was caught in a scandal when it was revealed that the company had installed software in millions of its diesel cars to cheat emissions tests. This 'defeat device' recognised when the cars were being tested and changed their performance accordingly to improve results; following the tests, they would revert to their standard settings and emit pollutants up to forty times above the allowable limit in the US.

This scandal severely tarnished Volkswagen's reputation, especially considering its efforts to portray itself as an environmentally friendly company. It led to billions of dollars in fines, the recall of millions of cars, and the resignation of the company's CEO. The crisis also significantly impacted Volkswagen's share price, led to a significant loss of trust among customers, shareholders and the public, and resulted in the company's ultimate agreement to pay compensation charges to some 91,000 British drivers that will come to over €200 million.

Risk assessment: What are potential sources of damage to the organisation's reputation, public image or brand that could be triggered by any one or a combination of the other crisis families? (e.g., negative publicity or media coverage; social media backlash; boycotts; ethical or legal controversies)

Risk mitigation:

a   **Public relations and engagement.** Invest in proactive measures, including comprehensive public relations campaigns, stakeholder involvement and corporate social responsibility programs (e.g., facing criticism and backlash over labour conditions in its supply chain, Nike released lists of its factories—which was an unprecedented move at the time—and launched campaigns to highlight its commitment to improving worker conditions and rights).

b   **Crisis recovery and reputation management.** Formulate and execute clear strategies post-crisis, encompassing corrective measures, public apologies and efforts toward restitution (e.g., after a passenger was forcibly removed from an overbooked flight in 2017, United Airlines swiftly undertook crisis recovery and reputation management efforts by revising overbooking policies, increasing compensation for voluntarily bumped passengers and ensuring employee retraining, in addition to issuing a public apology from United CEO Oscar Munoz and reaching a settlement with the affected passenger).

Communication: Designate spokespersons, key messages and communication channels in the event of a crisis.

Customising your template: Business model canvas

You will recall from the first chapter how we connected Osterwalder and Pigneur's Business Model Canvas [30] to the concept of situation awareness. By further connecting each component of that canvas to crisis family templates, we can better ensure that our organisation's crisis management strategies will align with its overarching business model. This alignment enables a comprehensive and resilient approach to wicked problems, as organisations are able to better anticipate, prepare for and respond to crises within each specific sector of their model.

Let's revisit each of the nine components of the Business Model Canvas, and see how wicked problem preparedness can be built into each.

Customer segments
Identify which of your customer segments would be most affected by each crisis family, and tailor crisis management strategies to address their needs, concerns and expectations. They should also be proactively communicated with about the status of the resolution and what the company is doing to prevent such a problem in the future.

Value propositions

Consider how each crisis family may impact your organisation's value propositions, and identify strategies for maintaining or enhancing them during and after a crisis. This could include improving product safety, ensuring service continuity or demonstrating corporate responsibility.

Channels

Evaluate the channels by which you communicate with your customers and stakeholders, and ensure that they are reliable, effective, and capable of delivering consistent messaging in the event of a crisis. Develop alternative media if necessary.

Customer relationships

Assess the impact of each crisis family on your customer relationships, and identify strategies to safeguard them in the event of a crisis. This could include proactive communication, providing support and resources, or offering special incentives.

Revenue streams

Analyse how each crisis family may affect the organisation's revenue streams, and develop contingency plans to minimise disruptions. This could include diversification, adjusting pricing strategies or exploring new market opportunities.

Key resources

Determine the critical resources required to manage and recover from each crisis family, such as skilled personnel, financial resources, technology or physical infrastructure. Ensure that these resources are accessible and well-maintained.

Key activities

Identify the critical activities for effective crisis management, such as risk assessment, contingency planning, communication and recovery efforts. Align these activities with the organisation's overall business processes and priorities.

Key partnerships

Evaluate the role of key partners in addressing each crisis family, including suppliers, distributors, emergency response agencies, industry associations, etc. Develop collaborative relationships and communication plans to ensure coordinated action during a crisis.

Cost structure

Consider the costs of managing and recovering from each crisis family, such as emergency response efforts, business disruption, reputational damage, etc. Develop strategies to minimise costs, optimise resource allocation and prioritise investments in crisis management.

As we did in the first chapter, we must now over-lay a Strategic Planning Framework to consider the external/environmental factors that can influence or impact the operation of our business model, and apply the same calculus of crisis family preparedness to them. These factors include:

Market forces. Consider how each crisis family could impact such things as customer preferences, market segments or demand.

Industry forces. How would each crisis family affect such factors as competition, value chain structure or industry dynamics? Assess your organisation's position within the industry, identify best practices or benchmarking opportunities for crisis management, and devise your crisis templates to incorporate industry-specific insights and leverage the organisation's competitive advantages during a crisis.

Macroeconomic forces. What effect would economic cycles, regulations, global events (e.g., a pandemic, the war in Ukraine), etc. have on each crisis family? Craft your templates to incorporate such factors as financial resilience, regulatory compliance or geopolitical risk mitigation.

Key trends. Analyse how each crisis family could impact such areas as technology, sociocultural factors or sustainability. Inform your crisis management templates with strategies that are forward-looking, adaptive and responsive to changing conditions and emerging challenges.

Customising your template: Empathy map

In the first chapter, we noted that the Business Model Canvas is intrinsically related to the Empathy Maps of our assorted customer segments in the context of situation awareness. Just as we did above, we can also prepare templates for wicked problems by analysing how each crisis family would impact the key areas of our customer empathy map.

As you'll recall, an Empathy Map consists of quadrants that represent different aspects of a customer's experience (Figure 4). To apply the crisis family templates to your Empathy Map:

1 Identify key customer segments that would be affected by each crisis family (e.g., end users, business partners, suppliers, other stakeholders).

2 Develop Empathy Maps for each customer segment.

a Evaluate the core customer emotions, concerns and motivations that would be impacted by each crisis family, and how this would be reflected back on the organisation.

b Identify the audio-visual evidence of each crisis family that customers may encounter, such as media coverage, social media posts or physical signs of disruption.

c Determine the likely messages and information customers may receive during a crisis, whether from the organisation, peers or other sources.

d   Analyse customers' likely actions in response to a crisis, including their communication with others and changes in their behaviour.

e   Identify customers' challenges, fears or frustrations during a crisis.

f   Recognise the opportunities for the organisation to provide support, reassurance or solutions that meet the customers' needs during a crisis.

3   Integrate customer insights from Empathy Maps into crisis management strategies.

a   Develop crisis communication plans that address different customer segments' information needs, emotions and concerns.

b   Implement support mechanisms to assist customers during a crisis, such as customer-service hotlines, dedicated crisis response teams or online resources.

c   Create strategies to rebuild customer trust and loyalty following a crisis, such as transparent updates on corrective actions, targeted marketing campaigns or special promotions.

By incorporating customer Empathy Maps into developing crisis family templates, organisations ensure a customer-centric approach to crisis management that addresses those customers' diverse needs and concerns. This approach not only helps mitigate the impact of crises on customers, but can also strengthen the organisation's long-term reputation and relationships with them.

CASE STUDY
Toyota and the Tōhoku disaster, 2011

The 2011 Tōhoku earthquake and tsunami was one of the most devastating natural disasters in history. It resulted in approximately 19,759 deaths, 6,242 people injured and 2,553 people missing and caused widespread destruction, with about one million buildings damaged or destroyed. The disaster also instigated a severe nuclear accident at the Fukushima Daiichi nuclear power plant, leading to radioactive contamination and the long-term displacement of nearby residents. The World Bank estimated the economic cost to be $235 billion, making it the costliest natural disaster on record.

Along with so many other areas of the economy, the disaster significantly impacted the global automotive supply chain, causing widespread disruption to car production and the availability of components [71]. Automotive market leader Toyota's response to the disaster demonstrates the value of using templating for crisis management. Among the items on their preparedness and response checklist were:

* **Risk assessment and mitigation.** Before the disaster, Toyota had implemented a supply chain risk management system that identified potential risks and vulnerabilities—

including the possibility of natural disasters—that allowed them to devise contingency plans and alternative sourcing strategies in case of a disruption.

- **Crisis response team.** When the disaster struck, Toyota's crisis response team was activated and quickly assessed the impact on the company's supply chain, coordinated recovery efforts, and communicated with suppliers, customers and other stakeholders.

- **Supplier support and recovery.** Toyota worked closely with its suppliers to assess the damage, provide financial aid and assist in recovery, using predefined templates so that they could focus on their most critical partners first.

- **Production adjustments and alternative sourcing.** Toyota adjusted its production schedules to minimise the impact of the supply chain disruption and leveraged its global supply network to source components from alternative suppliers, ensuring continuity of production.

- **Continuous improvement and learning.** After the crisis, Toyota thoroughly reviewed its response to the disaster, identifying lessons learned and areas for improvement. For example, Toyota reviewed all its suppliers, even the most indirect, giving it a better understanding of its supply chain and allowing it to react quicker in times of crisis. Toyota was the first automaker to adjust its supply chain management system from a purely 'just-in-time' model to a hybrid model, in which it stockpiles critical components such as semiconductors. Furthermore, most of its suppliers, including chipmakers, are Japanese companies, which prioritise supplying Toyota. The corporation also prioritises good relations with suppliers, and pledges not to renegotiate fees after a contract has been signed.

What these lessons and adjustments meant was that when COVID led to a global microchip shortage that squeezed the global auto industry, it barely dented Toyota's production. Where other global car makers were forced to revise production plans, Toyota exceeded its 2021 sales targets and expected to sell even more units in 2022.

Of course, Toyota's supply chain is not entirely disaster-proof. However, the goal of the company's crisis management templates is not to create an invulnerable supply chain—which is impossible anyway—but rather to enhance their resilience and ability to respond to such disasters with the utmost effectiveness.

CONCLUSION

Templates or checklists provide valuable structures when preparing for and addressing wicked problems. These tools are beneficial for detailing stakeholder identification, data collection protocols, progress tracking, and for managing smaller, linear tasks within the broader wicked problem. By breaking down complex issues into more manageable parts, they can guide brainstorming, facilitate systematic documentation of insights, decisions and plans, and ensure that critical considerations are not overlooked.

But it is crucial that these checklists or templates be developed out of a thorough, conventional process of risk assessment. The process of creating these tools can stimulate productive conversations and critical thinking about the problem at hand, encouraging teams to anticipate potential scenarios and prepare appropriate responses in advance. This fosters a proactive mindset, a crucial aspect when dealing with wicked problems.

However, the very nature of wicked problems—their complexity and unpredictability—demands more than a rigid adherence to a checklist or template. Effective management of such problems requires ongoing collaboration, open communication, creative problem-solving, and a readiness to adapt as the understanding of the problem evolves.

Let's remember Mike Tyson's words of wisdom: 'Everyone has a plan until they get punched in the mouth.' When a wicked problem is actually upon us, its complexity or chaos nakedly revealing all the overlooked flaws and fissures in our best laid plans, how do we adapt and continue to respond effectively in the heat of the moment? This question is at the core of our fifth SORTED Principle.

execution

Satya Nadella and Microsoft

When Satya Nadella became the CEO of Microsoft in 2014, the company's dominance in the PC market—where its Windows operating system and Office Suite had reigned supreme—was being significantly undermined. Shifts towards mobile computing and free or low-cost cloud-based software were threatening Microsoft's core business model. Internally, meanwhile, the company was plagued by a deeply ingrained culture of competition that discouraged collaboration and stifled innovation. There was no single solution to these intertwined issues; what the company required was a complex, comprehensive and flexible approach.

Nadella began with an internal cultural shift in which he aimed to transform a 'know-it-all' culture to a 'learn-it-all' one. This was a significant departure from the company's past and required convincing thousands of employees to embrace a new mindset. Nadella led by example and frequently spoke about the need for empathy, learning and collaboration.

Recognising and adapting to the shifts in the external technological landscape was also crucial, and Nadella accordingly refocused Microsoft's strategy from PCs towards cloud computing and artificial intelligence. This involved significant investments in building the Azure cloud platform and developing innovative AI technologies, all while competing with established players in the cloud market, like Amazon.

Another critical aspect of the problem was Microsoft's historical resistance to open source, which had isolated the company from a significant portion of the tech community. Nadella understood that this approach was no longer sustainable in an era where open-source technology was driving much of the industry's innovation. In a bold move, he led Microsoft to embrace open source, signalling a significant shift in the company's approach and philosophy.

Under Nadella's leadership, Microsoft also pursued strategic acquisitions, such as LinkedIn and

GitHub, and partnerships, even with long-standing competitors like Red Hat and Sony. Each of these moves was targeted at strengthening Microsoft's position in the changing tech landscape and required careful negotiation and integration efforts.

By 2021, Microsoft had seen a significant turnaround. Its culture was more collaborative, its product portfolio was diversified and aligned with market trends, and the company had achieved a prominent position in the cloud market. Its market capitalisation even surpassed $1 trillion, demonstrating the financial success of its strategic transformation.

A S THE EXAMPLE of Microsoft under Nadella's leadership illustrates, a crucial component of addressing a multifaceted wicked problem is the realisation that that conventional operational management approaches and preconceived solutions may not always hold the answer to such intricate issues. In this chapter, therefore, we will explore how leaders can equip themselves with both the mindset and the will to perceive the (sometimes dramatic) strategic pivots that wicked problems demand, and then execute those actions in order to seize the wicked opportunities these problems can present.

A central theme here is the need for a *bias for action*. Wicked problems call for more than theorising; they demand decisive, calculated steps towards tangible solutions. Despite the inherent uncertainties, it's through our actions that we make meaningful progress.

Fighting friction: Lessons from Clausewitz

At the end of the previous chapter, I quoted a famous epithet from Mike Tyson: 'Everyone has a plan until they get punched in the mouth.' But I suspect that Mr Tyson adapted that turn of phrase from an earlier saying: 'No plan survives contact with the enemy.' The phrase comes from *On War* [72] by Carl von Clausewitz, a 19th century Prussian military strategist and philosopher whose theories on planning in the context of warfare continue to be studied by both military and business strategists to this day.

Clausewitz's maxim derives from his larger concept of the 'fog of war'. This refers to the uncertainty, confusion and ambiguity that are inherent elements of military operations, and which make obtaining accurate information challenging—both in terms of the enemy's intentions and capabilities, and of the success of one's own battle strategy. This uncertainty creates what Clausewitz called 'friction', meaning the difference between the plan as conceived and its actual execution on the battlefield.

To minimise friction, Clausewitz advocated for a flexible, adaptable approach to planning, emphasising decentralised decision-making that allows commanders to adjust their tactics based on the evolving situation on the battlefield. He also stressed the significance of understanding the enemy's 'centre of gravity'—by which he meant the essential source of their power or will to continue fighting—

and making that centre the primary focus of attack, as this would directly affect the enemy's ability to wage war.

Undoubtedly, war constitutes a wicked problem in many respects, and Clausewitz's work is one of the reasons I advocate for *templates*, not detailed plans, when it comes to dealing with wicked problems. Templates allow for flexibility and adaptability in their execution, which better fits the dynamic and evolving nature of wicked problems. And the ability to properly execute in such situations demands a different kind of leadership than the day-to-day leadership of operational management.

Operational management is premised on:

- working exclusively within a specific sector of an organisation, such as production, finance or marketing;

- measuring performance and success via short-term metrics;

- addressing well-defined problems in which cause-and-effect relationships are transparent and predictable;

- pursuing problem-solving through proven methods and best practices; and

- favouring a risk-averse approach that prioritises stability and predictability.

By contrast, the kind of leadership required to execute in the event of a wicked problem—what I call *wicked leadership*—demands an entirely different kind of orientation, founded on:

- a comprehensive, systems-level understanding of the organisation's workings that traverses the boundaries of discrete departments;

- long-term strategic thinking that considers the future impacts of decisions made in the present;

- tackling complex and chaotic problems (i.e., wicked problems) that have multiple, dynamically interacting sources of causation and unpredictable effects;

- encouraging innovative, out-of-the-box thinking and novel approaches that may not have a proven track record of success; and

- embracing risk and uncertainty in problem-solving, and being prepared to change course when new events, information or insights emerge.

In the next section, we'll examine perhaps the key tenet of wicked leadership in the context of executing both decisively and adaptively when tackling a wicked problem: developing a *bias for action*.

A bias for action

An objective without a plan is just a wish; so too is a plan without action. Objectives and plans simply don't matter if you fail to act. Having a bias for action means that taking purposeful action is your default state. It's about focusing your energy and enthusiasm on execution, getting things done as simply and effectively as possible and then moving on to the next thing [73–76]. A bias for action is the natural progression of a template planning philosophy for dealing with wicked problems, because drilling down to an absurd level of detail is a waste of time since the situation changes the moment you act.

At the same time, however, having a bias for action doesn't mean 'just do it'. That kind of attitude can discount or ignore mitigating or complicating issues, whereas a genuine bias for action accounts for them. Conversely, having a bias for action is not about constantly doing everything you can; it's about *doing something purposeful and constructive* when confronted with an urgent and dynamic situation.

Those who have a bias for action [75]:

- Know who they are, and know their business;

- Are critical and realistic about their position at their business;

- Know the people they work with, and look to put the right people in the right place;

- Create a work environment that matches their ambitions, and clearly communicate their expectations of the people in that environment;

- Learn relentlessly themselves, and seek to expand their people's capabilities so that they can spark greatness in others;

- Identify clear goals and priorities, and follow through on the actions they initiate;

- Are neither frenzied or hasty, nor overly contemplative or analytical in their decision-making; and

- Are not fearful of failure, and approach challenges with a calm and reflective demeanour—particularly during times of crisis or chaos.

Developing a Bias for Action: Lessons from 'JW'
There are things you can do now to develop a bias for action [76]:

- First, *be mindful*—live in the present moment and focus. Visualise your intent; confront ambivalence.

- *Prepare for obstacles* and self-distance—if something seems insurmountable or you start overthinking, you're less likely to move and act. So, pause, mentally step outside, clear your mind, step back, and re-engage.

- *Break big problems down into smaller ones*, making for smaller decisions.

- *Make choices* by creating a 'decision system'. At its simplest, that's a diary and a to-do list linked to a planner. Plan annually, quarterly, monthly, weekly and daily—a little and often.

- Set *aspirational, experiential rewards* for success.

My favourite exemplar of a leader with a bias for action is one of my early mentors: John Williamson, or 'JW', as he is known to the colleagues who love him—and I don't use the word 'love' trivially. JW was my programme manager when I joined a large change management programme team at the Royal Bank of Scotland in London. Our task was relatively simple: move the complex credit data of two million customers from seven legacy systems to four new systems over a 48-hour period.

When we first met, JW was implacably and consistently ruthless in shaping me. In monitoring my work, his view was that he saw a latent ability in me, but that my approach was 'all wrong'. Rather than the snotty, over-opinionated academic with a superiority complex that, in hindsight, I realise I was, JW needed a commercially minded project manager who could solve problems and respond to client or project needs without letting ego get in the way of pragmatism.

Until JW 'polished' me, I would give clients all the reasons why I couldn't solve something, and several explanations of why the clients' proposed solutions couldn't possibly work. I spent too much time talking, not enough time listening, and nowhere near enough time thinking about practical solutions.

A straightforward exercise sharply refocused my mind. One day, JW permitted me to answer his questions strictly with 'yes', 'no', or 'I don't know'. A 'yes' or 'no' reply from me would spur an action for him or an instruction for me, while 'I don't know' brought a singular instruction: 'Well, go and find out then.' The exercise drove me slightly mad, and by the close of business that day I was busting for an argument. JW took one look at me and said, 'Right, down the pub then, for a chat.'

Later, over a beer, he explained the purpose of the exercise: 'Now you've learned to listen, ask questions, and come up with practical solutions instead of spouting rubbish without listening to what the client wants or finding their pain points.'

In hindsight, I realised that this was a master class in developing a bias for action as well as critical thinking. While superficially brutal, it was truly what Susan Scott calls a fierce conversation [77], and it's a lesson that has stuck to this day. What JW did was to open my mindset, moving me from 'telling' to 'listening' and from 'reacting' to 'acting'. For an academic who was used to the slightly artificial world of higher education, where there are rarely serious consequences for poor performance, JW made my work 'real': he forced me to engage in my work mindfully, confronting challenges, listening deeply, and understanding that there are consequences in the real world of work. In short, he trained me to be active rather than reactive.

I wasn't singled out, by the way. JW mentored everyone on his team, including my friends and colleagues Mike, Basharit, Mark and Iftikhar, all of whom benefited in different ways from JW's attention. Such was his impact on us that we became his core team, and although we were all independent, we followed him around jobs after RBS. Those colleagues each went on to have successful careers in programme management in a variety of sectors, and I doubt they would have enjoyed the level of success that they did without JW's attention.

A Bias for Action and Wicked Problems

A bias for action is a valuable leadership quality for tackling wicked problems in several ways. It encourages experimentation and iterative problem-solving, which allows teams to test different strategies, learn from failures and refine their solutions. This trial-and-error approach promotes continuous learning and improvement, which is essential for overcoming the uncertainty and complexity of wicked problems.

A bias for action drives leaders to make timely decisions and execute them, even when the available information is imperfect or incomplete. Action helps overcome analysis paralysis and creates momentum towards a solution. It promotes collaboration and engagement with diverse stakeholders, fostering dialogue and building trust. It also inspires commitment from team members and stakeholders by demonstrating progress through concrete actions.

Furthermore, it encourages leaders to remain agile and responsive to change, proactively seek out and mobilise resources, and cultivate a problem-solving culture within their teams and organisations. By focusing on these aspects, leaders develop a bias for action that enables them to tackle complex, interconnected challenges effectively.

CASE STUDY
Alan Mulally & Ford

When Alan Mulally became CEO of the Ford Motor Company in 2006, the auto maker was struggling with declining market share, mounting losses and a disjointed product portfolio [79]. The global financial crisis further exacerbated these difficulties, pushing the entire automotive industry towards the brink of collapse. Ford's wicked problem involved multiple interconnected challenges, including the need to revitalise its product lineup, restructure its operations and navigate the financial crisis.

Under Mulally's leadership, Ford executed a remarkable turnaround by focusing on a set of key strategies:

- **'One Ford' plan.** Mulally developed and executed a comprehensive plan to unify Ford's global operations and product development by emphasising a more cohesive brand identity, streamlining the product lineup and fostering collaboration across divisions. The plan allowed

Ford to leverage economies of scale, share resources and capitalise on its global footprint.

- **Focus on core brands.** Ford divested non-core brands, such as Jaguar, Land Rover, Aston Martin and Volvo, to concentrate its resources and attention on its core Ford and Lincoln brands. This strategic decision helped the company invest in developing more competitive and appealing products.

- **Investment in quality and fuel efficiency.** Understanding the growing importance of environmental concerns to consumers, Mulally invested heavily in research and development to improve the fuel efficiency and quality of Ford's products, eventually introducing innovative technologies like EcoBoost engines and electric vehicles.

- **Restructuring and cost reduction.** Ford undertook a significant restructuring effort, including workforce reductions, renegotiating labour contracts and consolidating manufacturing facilities, to help reduce costs and improve operational efficiency.

- **Financial management.** Using the company's assets as collateral, Mulally secured a $23.6 billion loan in 2006 that gave Ford the necessary liquidity to weather the financial crisis and invest in its turnaround plan without resorting to government bailouts like its competitors, General Motors and Chrysler.

- **Culture change.** Mulally instilled a culture of transparency, collaboration and accountability through such initiatives as weekly business plan review meetings, where all major divisions shared progress updates and discussed challenges. The change helped break down silos and foster a problem-solving mentality throughout the organisation.

The result of these efforts was a remarkable turnaround for Ford. By 2009, the company posted profits and gained market share, even as its competitors struggled. Moreover, Ford's stock price increased significantly during Mulally's tenure, reflecting the successful execution of his strategy in the face of a wicked problem.

Mulally's strategic leadership and bias for action underlines the importance of execution in addressing complex business challenges. His 'One Ford' Plan signified a deep understanding of global operational complexities and a vision of a unified, more efficient company. His decision to concentrate resources on core brands and divest non-essential ones demonstrated a disciplined approach to resource allocation, embodying his philosophy of 'doing fewer things better'.

Further, by investing in research and development focused on fuel efficiency and quality, Mulally showcased his ability to anticipate market trends and consumer needs, aligning Ford with the rising environmental consciousness. The restructuring and cost reduction efforts displayed his strategic acumen and ability to navigate the intricacies of a competitive marketplace while maintaining beneficial relations with external stakeholders.

Securing a $23.6 billion loan using company assets as collateral was a testament to Mulally's financial prowess and his capacity to take calculated risks to ensure Ford's survival and growth. Lastly, his commitment to transforming Ford's organisational culture, fostering transparency and collaboration, underlined the importance he placed on culture as a catalyst in strategy execution.

Mulally's leadership at Ford highlights how a combination of analytical thinking and decisive action can lead a company to a successful turnaround in the face of extreme adversity.

CONCLUSION

In this chapter, we delved into the critical aspects of addressing wicked problems, emphasising the significance of adaptability and flexibility in devising solutions to them. One key insight was that traditional operational management approaches might not always be the most effective in tackling wicked problems; instead, they often require leadership skills specifically tailored to address the unique demands of wicked problems and seize the opportunities they present. Understanding that these issues require a different approach and mindset means empowering individuals with the right skill set to navigate through the intricacies and uncertainties they entail.

A pivotal concept I highlighted was the necessity of having a *bias for action* when it comes to implementing solutions for wicked problems. It is not enough to merely analyse and theorise; action is the driving force that propels us towards tangible outcomes. Taking calculated and decisive steps, even in the face of ambiguity, becomes the catalyst for making progress.

Having engaged with the wicked problem or opportunity, the next crucial question arises: What is the path forward from here? How do we proceed in further developing solutions and enhancing our problem-solving skills in the context of wicked problems?

development

McDonald's, 2000-23

Since its founding in 1940, McDonald's has grown into one of the world's largest and most recognisable fast-food chains. However, for decades it has struggled with its decidedly mixed reputation among the public due to factors related to its products, operations and business practices [78, 79]. These include:

- its calorie-dense menu items, which have been linked to health issues such as obesity, heart disease and diabetes

- its labour practices, including low wages, lack of benefits and exploitative working conditions

- its negative environmental impact, mainly related to waste generation, deforestation (due to beef and palm oil sourcing), and excessive energy and water consumption

- its animal welfare practices, particularly concerning factory farming and the inhumane treatment of animals in its supply chain

While the company had shown an ability to defensively adapt aspects of its business model in the face of public criticism, it started addressing its problem issues in earnest in the early 2000s, taking more proactive measures to mitigate the adverse effects of its operations and, consequently, to improve its reputation. Some of these measures included:

- establishing a Global Animal Health and Welfare Team, and working with leading animal welfare experts to develop guidelines and auditing systems for its suppliers

- in response to customer demand for healthier choices, expanding their menu to include such items as premium salads, fruit, yoghurt and grilled chicken

- becoming the first global restaurant company to adopt a sustainable fisheries policy, and continuing to improve its sourcing practices in areas like beef, palm oil and coffee

- launching an energy efficiency program to reduce restaurant energy consumption, and setting ambitious goals for sustainable packaging and recycling

- implementing wage increases for workers at company-owned restaurants in the United States (although this did not apply to the franchise restaurants that comprise most McDonald's locations)

The company's efforts to address its multi-pronged wicked reputational problem have continued to develop into the 2020s, through such initiatives as a commitment to using 100% renewable, recyclable or certified materials in all its packaging by 2025; introducing plant-based food items; investing in energy-efficient technologies and green building designs; establishing a Sustainable Agriculture Policy and issuing annual sustainability reports; and more.

W HILE MCDONALD'S still faces public challenges to its practices—at the time of writing, the company's board is struggling with board member and well-known private equity investor Carl Icahn over its apparent inability to eliminate the usage of cruel pig gestation crates in its supply chain [80]—the fast-food giant offers an exemplary case of a company developing, expanding and innovating its decades-tested template for success in response to internal and external challenges.

In this chapter, I delve into the enhancement of templated solutions and the development of wicked problem-solving skills through experiential learning at both individual and organisational levels. I begin by examining how organisations recover from wicked problems, exploring the *critical curves* they navigate during crises and the strategies they employ at pivotal moments. This understanding of critical curves provides valuable insights into the pathways to recovery and resilience in the face of complex challenges.

Furthermore, I explore the concept of building *reliably safe organisations* that possess the capacity to effectively handle future wicked problems and capitalise on emerging opportunities. These organisations prioritise safety and reliability, incorporating robust processes and systems to prevent crises and mitigate their impacts.

A key aspect that emerges from this exploration is the significance of *psychological safety* within organisations. To address wicked problems arising from *volatile, uncertain, complex and ambiguous* (VUCA) environments, leaders must foster an environment where team members feel psychologically secure, which, in turn, encourages them to practice *provocative competence*, confidently challenging prevailing assumptions and proposing innovative solutions.

Throughout the chapter, the emphasis lies on experiential learning, wherein organisations and individuals actively learn from their experiences in tackling wicked problems. This learning process helps them adapt, evolve and continuously improve their problem-solving skills, making them better prepared for future challenges.

Critical curves: Recovering (or not) from wicked problems

Let's now look at how organisations and businesses attempt to carry on in the wake of the wicked problems that have disrupted their everyday operations—some of which are more effective than others, depending on the nature of the particular wicked problem that they face.

Typically, organisations hit with a wicked problem hew to one of five 'critical curves' (Figure 6).

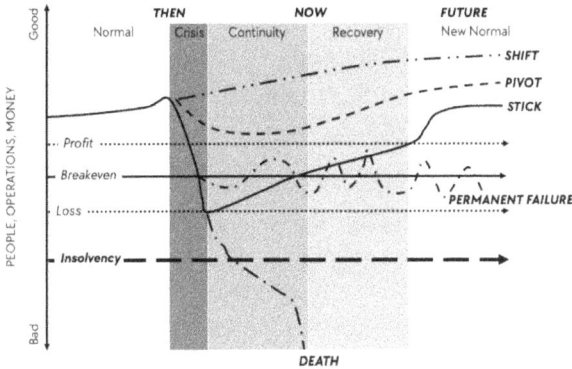

FIGURE 6 Critical curves

A company may move into continuity, recovery and a 'new' normal, depending on their response:

1   A *shift* strategy means looking for new customer segments and making substantial changes in cost drivers and other factors that drive revenue. Shifts are radical solutions wherein the move to the new normal is usually immediately positive.

2   If businesses *pivot* strategically, performance will dip but recover rapidly. There are two types of pivot strategy—to new customer segments or making substantial changes in cost drivers and other factors that drive revenue.

3   A *stick* strategy means sticking with existing customers and making minimal changes to other business model elements. It leads to less-certain outcomes. Indeed, it sounds like the standard definition of madness, i.e., doing the same thing repeatedly and expecting a different result. Sticking for most companies leads to financial difficulty, but they may recover as the problem eases due to external influences.

4   Other businesses with no clear strategy (not even 'stick') permanently fail (the organisational equivalent of a persistent vegetative state). Their existence continues more by luck than judgement.

Organisational death ensues for a minority following a 'stick' strategy [16, 81].

Having explored the diverse responses of organisations to wicked problems, I now look at the strategies they employ to improve their solutions and adapt to the aftermath of disruption. *Continuous improvement* and *radical innovation* emerge as two distinct approaches that organisations may adopt to navigate the critical curves and pave their path forward.

Improving templated solutions: Continuous improvement or radical innovation?

Continuous improvement involves a systematic and incremental approach to refining existing processes, products and strategies. By analysing past experiences and learning from the challenges they faced, organisations can make gradual adjustments to enhance their problem-solving capabilities. This method is well-suited for organisations that opt for a 'stick' strategy, as it allows them to optimise their existing business model and adapt incrementally to changing circumstances.

Conversely, *radical innovation* offers a more daring and transformative approach. Organisations pursuing a 'shift' strategy may embrace radical innovation by exploring new customer segments, reimagining revenue drivers, and implementing substantial changes in their cost structures. This audacious approach can yield immediate positive results, propelling the organisation towards a 'new normal' that is better equipped to handle future wicked problems.

Businesses that pivot strategically, either by targeting new customer segments or making significant changes in cost drivers and revenue factors, may experience temporary performance dips but can bounce back rapidly. This aligns with both continuous improvement and radical innovation, as it enables organisations to adapt swiftly and effectively to the evolving landscape.

However, the risks are high for those that stick rigidly to their existing customers and business model without incorporating meaningful changes. This 'stick' strategy may lead to financial difficulty and, in some cases, even organisational death. Organisations in this position must recognise the need for transformation and consider either continuous improvement or radical innovation to break free from the cycle of uncertainty.

I now examine how organisations implement these approaches to enhance their resilience, overcome the disruptive effects of wicked problems, and create a pathway towards sustainable growth. By embracing the concepts of continuous improvement and radical innovation, organisations can build adaptive capacities, bolster problem-solving capabilities and thrive in the face of wicked challenges.

Continuous improvement

As per its name, continuous improvement involves an ongoing effort to refine and enhance processes, systems and solutions over time, and evaluating the results of those changes to drive further improvements [82]. Given that wicked problems are complex, multifaceted challenges that are often resistant to simple solutions, creating effective templates for addressing these problems requires consistent iteration, learning and adaptation. This allows organisations to identify areas where these solutions have been proven to fall short, and adjust them so that they can better remain effective and impactful as the problems they seek to address evolve.

Those leading the charge on templated solutions should seek feedback (via surveys, focus groups or interviews) from those using their templates in the field. By listening to the input of those on the ground, developers gain valuable insights into how their templates work in practice. In addition, developers should analyse data on their templates' use by measuring metrics for such things as adoption rates, completion times or user satisfaction scores to identify patterns and trends that might suggest areas for improvement.

Based on the results of their evaluations, developers should trial-run different versions of the template with tweaks to its structure, format, wording, etc. with the goal of making them more intuitive, user-friendly or practical. In addition to making changes to the templates themselves, developers may provide additional training and support to users through such means as more detailed instructions, one-on-one coaching, or materials like videos or webinars.

The new iterations of the template should then be subjected to the same evaluation processes as in the first step, monitoring such metrics as adoption rates, completion times or user satisfaction scores to see if the changes have had a positive effect.

Developers should stay up to date on new research or best practices in the field that is relevant to their template through such means as reading industry publications, attending conferences or webinars, or networking with other practitioners. In addition, they should engage in regular professional development activities (e.g., courses or workshops, mentorship or coaching from experienced practitioners, or pursuing advanced degrees or certifications), and actively seek feedback (from template users, colleagues or mentors) to identify areas for growth.

As per the steps above, continuous improvement is most often effective when it is a collaborative effort that seeks input from a diverse range of stakeholders. This might involve engagement with template users via surveys, focus groups or interviews; consulting academics, researchers or other subject matter experts; or working with other organisations or field practitioners who address similar wicked problems. Developers should also seek to incorporate diverse perspectives into their work, by engaging with stakeholders who have traditionally been marginalised or underrepresented in the field or seeking feedback from users from various backgrounds and experiences. This can help ensure that templates are effective for a range of users and communities.

As the context in which wicked problems arise constantly evolves, those working on templated solutions to them must be prepared to adapt to these changing circumstances. Developers should be willing to challenge their own assumptions, be open to new approaches that may prove more effective in addressing wicked problems, and be ready and able to pivot quickly if their initial solutions prove ineffective.

CASE STUDY
Johnson & Johnson Tylenol
tampering crisis, 1982

In 1982, Johnson & Johnson faced a grave crisis when seven people in Chicago died after consuming cyanide-laced Tylenol capsules. The company swiftly responded with a commitment to consumer safety, enacting a recall of all 31 million Tylenol bottles from store shelves in the US. Led by CEO James Burke, the company maintained transparent communication with the public, media and authorities, while conducting a thorough investigation in collaboration with law enforcement agencies to identify the source of contamination.

While this is an exemplary case of crisis response in the face of a wicked problem, Johnson & Johnson did not stop there. Rather than merely reintroducing the same product, the company used the crisis as an opportunity for continuous improvement by introducing tamper-evident, triple-sealed packaging, which set new industry standards for consumer safety. Additionally, Johnson & Johnson worked closely with regulators to enhance safety guidelines for over-the-counter drugs.

By prioritising transparency, innovation and adherence to its values, Johnson & Johnson not only resolved the crisis effectively, but also strengthened its brand and reputation in the long run, setting a benchmark for continuous improvement in crisis response.

Radical innovation

At the other end of the spectrum from continuous improvement is radical innovation, which involves exploring new and different ways of applying templated solutions or creating entirely new templates to address these complex challenges [83, 84].

One way to explore new applications of templated solutions is to adapt existing templates to new contexts or problem domains. For example, 'Healthy Kids, Happy Planet', which started as a school-based public health initiative focused on improving children's eating habits, has now expanded its template to address the larger issue of food sustainability in communities, encouraging people to make eco-friendly food choices, supporting local farmers and reducing food waste. By repurposing successful strategies from the public health template, the program effectively addresses a broader social issue and contributes to a healthier environment for all.

Another method to tackle wicked problems is by combining existing templates to address complex challenges that span multiple fields. An example is the UNDP's Smart Cities initiative, which brings together templates from urban planning, environmental sustainability and technology integration to create innovative and efficient city designs. By combining these templates, cities can address issues related to transportation, energy consumption, waste management and public services in a holistic manner.

Additionally, developers can apply existing templates to new technologies or platforms, making wicked-problem solutions more accessible and impactful. For instance, Free Basics by Meta aims to provide free access to essential online services and information, making the internet more accessible to people in developing regions. Through partnerships with mobile network operators, 'Internet.org' offers free access to a selection of websites, including educational resources, health information, job portals and communication platforms. This approach enables people to access valuable online services without incurring data charges, thereby bridging the digital divide and providing opportunities for socio-economic development.

Conversely, developers can design a template from scratch when facing a highly unique and unprecedented challenge that existing templates cannot fully address. For instance, when dealing with a rapidly evolving global health crisis like a novel virus outbreak, a tailored template might be the preferable option due to the urgency and complexity of the situation.

One way to develop new templates is to draw on emerging research to create innovative solutions. For instance, researchers studying sustainable agriculture might uncover ground-breaking methods to optimise crop yields while preserving the environment. This new research can serve as the foundation for a whole new template that promotes eco-friendly and productive farming practices.

Another method is to leverage cutting-edge technologies or techniques, such as artificial intelligence

(AI), machine learning and data analytics, to develop solutions that were previously unattainable. For example, in disaster response, AI-powered algorithms can process vast amounts of data from various sources in real-time, enabling quicker and more precise decision-making and providing a template for more efficient disaster management.

These new concepts should then be prototyped, via basic versions of the proposed templates that are designed to test specific aspects of their functionality and effectiveness. The findings and feedback from this experimentation process are then used to inform successive iterations of the template, which are progressively upscaled to gauge how they would function in a real-life wicked-problem scenario.

As with continuous improvement, radical innovation should ideally involve a degree of collaboration, up to and including co-creation. Co-designing and co-developing a template with subject matter experts, potential users or interested parties in related fields can enable a more rapid and effective process of prototyping, testing and refining the proposed solution, and also potentially broaden its applicability across a range of fields.

For example, Google's Project Loon exemplifies radical innovation through collaboration and co-creation. The initiative aimed to provide internet connectivity to remote and underserved regions, or during crises, using high-altitude balloons. Engineers, scientists and experts from different fields collaborated to design and develop the complex communication system. Through extensive testing and prototyping, the team refined the solution and addressed technical challenges.

The collaborative approach also allowed the project to expand beyond its initial goal, as the balloons were used in disaster response to provide emergency communication networks. Project Loon's success has significantly impacted internet accessibility in isolated communities, empowering them with educational resources and economic opportunities. This example demonstrates the power of radical innovation achieved through collaborative efforts.

Building reliably safe organisations

'Success has a thousand fathers, but failure is an orphan,' the famous saying goes. But when dealing with wicked problems—which are, by definition, complex and resistant to traditional problem-solving methods—failures can provide valuable learning opportunities. Failures that result from genuine, thoughtful effort (as opposed to errors that arise from wild experimentation [85]) allow leaders to examine the assumptions behind their original actions, and provide data and insights that may not have been available through other means. By sharing and learning from each other's experiences, leaders and team members can guard their organisation against future, potentially more severe failures. This is how to build *reliably safe organisations* (also known as 'high-reliability organisations', or HROs).

A reliably safe organisation is built on a foundation of continuous learning at both the leadership and execution levels, the better to deal with three of the main organisational factors that can contribute to the amplification of wicked problems: *dynamic and hyper-complex environments*, *tight coupling* and *extreme hierarchical differentiation*. Let's quickly examine each of these in turn.

- *Dynamic and hyper-complex environments* are challenging and rapidly changing situations with intricate and unpredictable interactions among various elements. For example, a healthcare emergency room operates under constantly changing conditions, requiring staff to respond promptly to various medical issues. On the other hand, a space exploration mission involves multiple subsystems, technical dependencies and strict timelines, making it a hyper-complex operational setting. In both cases, HROs rely on high-reliability principles and safety culture to navigate uncertainty and maintain operational excellence.

- *Tight coupling* refers to a situation in which a small, seemingly insignificant event can quickly cascade into a much larger, catastrophic event due to the interdependence of various components or subsystems within a complex system. For example, tight coupling in a complex system can be seen in the aviation industry during aircraft operations. A minor mechanical failure during take-off, if not managed properly, can trigger a chain of events leading to a catastrophic situation. Interconnected issues such as disrupted control surfaces and communication problems can quickly escalate, compromising the aircraft's safety and control, highlighting the need for robust design and redundant systems in complex environments.

- *Extreme hierarchical differentiation* describes an organisational structure in which there is a high degree of separation between the stratum of management and employees, with decision-making authority sitting primarily at the top. This can hinder the flow of information by making it difficult for lower-level employees to either report potential problems or suggest improvements, creating an overall lack of organisational situation awareness that can impede the organisation's ability to respond swiftly and effectively to unexpected crises.

Throughout this book, I've repeatedly stressed the importance of building systems, processes and organisational learning mechanisms into the operations of a business. Reporting procedures, deadlines, chains of accountability and the like are essential for any complex organisation. But the kind of organisations I'm sketching in the list above have the tendency to make these *support structures* into their raison d'être—self-fulfilling, easily legible, and often wholly artificial benchmarks that provide a fabricated sense of accomplishment for anxious managers. Moreover, when adhered to solely for their own sake, such structures quash the critical thinking we must draw on to spot and tame wicked problems.

In a reliably safe organisation, these crisis-amplifying factors are nullified by a number of mechanisms born out of a culture of continuous learning. These include:

- *Redundant control and information systems* that support many decision-makers in complex communication networks at various hierarchical levels, and supported by a culture of continuous learning, addresses crisis-amplifying factors effectively. Redundant systems provide flexibility, enabling agile responses to unexpected events and preventing small disruptions from escalating. Swift and comprehensive information flow empowers decision-makers at various levels, promoting decentralised decision-making. The diversity of perspectives ensures creative problem-solving and reduces the risk of groupthink. Furthermore, by fostering a learning-oriented environment, organisations can identify vulnerabilities from past crises, leading to more robust systems.

- A *strong culture of accountability* ensures that high performance and adherence to standard procedures are valued and encouraged. Team members

are empowered to take ownership of their responsibilities, knowing that their contributions play a
crucial role in the organisation's success. When
accountability is prioritised, it fosters a sense of
responsibility and dedication among employees,
inspiring them to consistently strive for excellence.
This collaborative commitment to accountability not only promotes reliability and safety, but
also instils a shared desire to achieve the organisation's goals with confidence and competence.

- *Encouraging a streamlined decision-making process with prompt feedback* fosters a responsive and
agile work environment. By reducing decision-
making time, teams can quickly assess situations
and implement effective solutions. Immediate
feedback allows for continuous improvement
and empowers individuals to fine-tune their
approaches based on real-time results. For example, in a customer-service setting, frontline rep-
resentatives are empowered to make on-the-spot
decisions to resolve customer issues promptly.
They receive immediate feedback on the effectiveness of their actions, enabling them to adapt
and enhance their approach in real-time to ensure
customer satisfaction. In such an environment,
the emphasis is on enabling employees to make
well-informed decisions efficiently, promoting
a sense of ownership and confidence in their
abilities. This collaborative approach not only promotes reliability and efficiency but also cultivates

a culture of learning and adaptability, where teams thrive in delivering exceptional results.

- A *maximisation of autonomy* by which leaders strike an optimal balance between operational constraint (i.e., the structures and guidelines necessary to maintain a functional organisation) and an encouragement of *positive deviance*—i.e., the freedom for team members to question, depart from, or experiment with standard operating procedures. Too much consensus is as dangerous as no consensus at all, because it drives out variety and diverse ideas. The key is to have *just enough consensus* (primarily on the core mission and objectives of the organisation) rather than demanding universal agreement on every principle.

'Say yes to the mess': Reliable safety through provocative competence

That last point above is perhaps the most crucial one of all for building a reliably safe organisation. Instead of guarding against dissent and debate, leaders should value these things. Leaders must expand their vocabulary of how to say 'yes' rather than indulging in the effortless ego trip of saying 'no'. By encouraging positive deviance within a team and celebrating even the small successes and early wins that result from it, leaders enhance the efficacy of the group. Team members will expect more from each other, and will also likely have more faith in their team-mates' skills and capacities.

So then, how do you foster an environment where this kind of critical thinking can play freely without descending into anarchy? As Frank Barrett puts it, you 'say yes to the mess' [85].

The first critical step is to *level status differences* so people feel safe to experiment. We should frame our proposed solutions to problems as *experiments*, as a testing of our assumptions against a concrete situation that could either prove, disprove or qualify them. Influential change leaders must let others see them as fellow learners, and be among the first to admit mistakes. Demonstrating leadership this way means you are uncommonly receptive to whatever emerges. Defensive attitudes do not permit success-ful experimentation: by maintaining awareness of the constraints that your biases place upon your crit-ical thinking, you will be better able to detect those constraints in the thought of others.

Next, leaders should seek to *nurture a culture of spontaneity and improvisation*. Better execution comes from frequent 'play'—leaders might even consider calling 'time-outs' for play by incorporat-ing dedicated time into the work schedule for team members to brainstorm ideas, experiment with new approaches, or work on passion projects that are outside the scope of their regular work (with the pro-viso that these are all aligned with the organisation's ultimate goal). They should then encourage team members to share the ideas and insights they've gleaned from these activities, and provide constructive feedback and support to them.

Creating this kind of 'safe space' provides team members with *psychological safety* that promotes learning. Psychological safety is a concept developed by Amy Edmondson [86] that refers to the belief that one can express oneself without fear of negative consequences to self-image, status or career. It is feeling safe to take interpersonal risks, such as speaking up with ideas, questions or concerns, without fear of being judged, embarrassed or punished. In a psychologically safe work environment, team members feel comfortable expressing their opinions, asking for help and admitting mistakes. As a result, they are more likely to engage in open and honest communication, which leads to better problem-solving and innovation. Psychological safety is essential for effective collaboration, especially in teams dealing with complex and uncertain situations where mistakes have serious consequences.

A psychologically safe workplace is not one premised on an *absence* of conflict or tension; rather, it is an environment where people can work through challenges constructively and respectfully, and willingly listen to others' perspectives. When team members feel psychologically safe, they are more likely to share knowledge, ask questions and take risks, leading to better decision-making, increased innovation and improved overall performance.

Safe spaces can be created by something as simple as deliberately breaking a routine. Even a simple question posed during a team activity (e.g., 'I'm thinking we should talk about what we're doing here. What if we try something else?') can disrupt our perhaps stagnant 'normal' and trigger team members to consider other options. Thinking like this is a small way to break up a practice that might have become habituated and is handicapping performance outside of anyone's awareness.

Creating these kinds of safe spaces encourages a culture of 'jamming'—hanging out, sharing stories, tossing around ideas and thinking out loud (occasionally at considerable volume)—which is a proven generator of valuable new ideas. To return to our earlier example of Pixar, the free and open critique the company encourages is not simply the province of the 'Braintrust', but of all of its employees, who are encouraged to congregate informally and exchange ideas and insights, resulting in a vibrant and creative atmosphere where inspiration can strike from unexpected sources.

At the same time, you must channel free flow to gain the maximum amount of insight from your teams. Leaders must ensure that everyone has a chance to speak from time to time by developing a non-negotiable structure that monitors airtime, cultivates group creativity, and ensures that every individual has a voice. Developing that notion further, leaders improve teamwork by supporting behaviours such as mentoring, advocating, encouraging and listening. Promoting voice means rewarding those who support other people's opportunity to take centre stage. We need to help them as they transition and develop ideas at different rates, progressively blending into the group. As Frank Barrett puts it, 'Leaders celebrate teamwork to create a culture of noble followership' [85].

As leaders celebrate teamwork and noble followership, they also encourage another concept developed by Frank Barrett: *provocative competence.* Provocative competence refers to the ability to challenge prevailing assumptions, beliefs and norms in a constructive fashion, asking questions and making statements that stimulate thought and discussion while also respecting the opinions of others [85]. It is much more than simply 'disrupting' the work environment: rather, it entails calibrating the size of the challenge you are willing to embrace. In other words, individuals with provocative competence do not aim to create chaos or upheaval in the work environment, but rather to stimulate thought and discussion by respectfully questioning prevailing assumptions and beliefs.

Leaders can encourage provocative competence by evoking higher values and ideals that inspire passionate engagement and assessing team members' performance against those, essentially leveraging self-efficacy. Reliably safe organisations make expansive promises that defy reasonable limits, and thus stretch their employees to redefine the boundaries within which they have traditionally operated.

CONCLUSION

In this chapter, we focused on improving templated solutions and enhancing wicked problem-solving skills through experiential learning on both an individual and organisational level. I began by exploring how organisations recover from wicked problems by analysing critical curves, the paths they traverse through crises, and the strategies they adopt at pivotal moments. Understanding these critical curves provides valuable insights into fostering recovery and building resilience in the face of complex challenges.

We then delved into the practice of constructing *reliably safe organisations* that are equipped to effectively tackle future wicked problems and seize emerging opportunities. By prioritising safety and implementing robust processes, these organisations can prevent crises and mitigate their impacts, laying a foundation for sustained success.

Throughout this exploration, the significance of *psychological safety* within organisations emerged as a critical factor. To address wicked problems arising from volatile, uncertain, complex and ambiguous (VUCA) environments, leaders must foster a psychologically safe culture that empowers individuals to practice *provocative competence*, confidently challenging existing assumptions and proposing innovative solutions.

As we move into the final section of this book, our focus will shift towards the idea of *wicked leadership*, in recognition of the fact that addressing and taming wicked problems requires visionary and adaptive leaders who can navigate complexities and inspire teams to achieve shared goals. We will see how truly wicked leaders can embrace uncertainty, inspire innovation, and nurture a dynamic environment where individuals and teams thrive in the face of wicked challenges. By embracing these principles, organisations can truly become pioneers in solving complex problems and shaping a better future.

Closing Thoughts
On Wicked Leadership

THROUGHOUT THIS BOOK, I've discussed several ways to develop specific skills to help spot and tame wicked problems. Now it's time to bring it all together and answer the question: What does a *wicked leader* look like?

Six key characteristics define wicked leaders:

1 They practice *mindfulness*.

2 They *build on their personality and character strengths*.

3 They have a *growth mindset*.

4 They are *mentally tough*.

5 They can enter a *flow state* in demanding situations (such as dealing with a wicked problem).

6 Finally, they dedicate themselves to *lifelong learning*.

Here's the good news: wicked leaders are *made*, not born. The qualities above are not inherent in a blessed few—we can learn each through conscious effort. It's largely a matter of learning how to manage your *state*.

As we saw in the chapter on situation awareness, your *state* comprises what's going on in both your mind and body, as the two are intimately interconnected [181]. Its foundation is the belief that how we react to what life presents us is a matter of *choice* [87, 88]. As my mentor Matt Church and his colleagues put it in their invaluable book on public speaking [23]: 'The key is to be able to *respond* rather than *react*. To choose who and how you will be.'

Bringing and maintaining an energetic, engaging version of yourself to life in a way that feels genuinely authentic is challenging, but crucial for a wicked leader. As the head of your team, you set the energy for everyone else—which means that, by managing your state, you create the conditions for your team members to manage theirs.

That said, very few of us can simply 'choose' our state without consciously developing our ability to do so. This is precisely what those six characteristics above are: they are *active, mutually reinforcing, conscious practices* that allow us to manage our state better and, in doing so, prepare us for the challenge of facing and taming wicked problems.

Let's look at each one of them in turn.

Mindfulness

Taming wicked problems requires focus. Our focus is sharpest when we make the best use of our energy and time to live in the present, learn from it, and strive to be better tomorrow—a practice known as *mindfulness*. Achieving this requires an open-hearted awareness of our thoughts, emotions, bodily sensations and environment [89]—or, as I like to put it, an integration of your *body*, *mind* and *inputs*.

Body

At its most fundamental level, mindfulness is about *achieving discipline through bodily self-regulation*. First, proper sleep prepares our bodies for exercise, allowing our metabolism to slow and rejuvenate our bodies. Second, our diet fuels exercise and, according to our genotype, supports the health of our body's vital subsystems. Third, diet influences sleep: during sleep, the nutrients we ingest restore our body's systems and function [90-92]. Finally, just like cars, our bodies need proper servicing to run correctly.

Taking care of these physiological needs is the first step. From here, we need to learn how to feel truly *present* in our bodies. Here's a straightforward technique for achieving this [89]:

1 **Focus** very deliberately on your breathing for a few moments.

2 **Practise concentration**. Don't let disturbances into your head as you draw breath. Shut out any noise.

3 **Be aware of your body** as you draw breath. As your breathing evens out, you become more peaceful, and so does your body.

4 **Release tension.** Whatever you're moving towards, and indeed whatever it is you've come from, let it go.

Mind

Once we feel truly present in our bodies, we have set ourselves up for the next stage: self-awareness, that is, the capacity to recognise our feelings, behaviours and characteristics [93]. Self-awareness means that you consciously or non-consciously ask yourself: who am I, what do I want, what do I think, and how do I feel (physically and emotionally)?

Consider the following parable:[4]

A monk out walking hears the sound of a galloping horse. He turns to see a man riding a horse in his direction. When the man comes closer, the monk asks: 'Where are you going?' The man replies: 'I don't know, ask the horse,' and rides away.

The horse in the story represents your subconscious mind, which runs your existing mental model. It conditions your responses to your situation and environment [14, 94]. When you become more self-aware, you become better at decision-making because you are more conscious of your mental model and examine it critically.

---

4 https://www.outofstress.com/self-realization-short-stories/ accessed 28 June 2022

Increasing your self-awareness means that you are better able to *gain perspective*. Increasing self-awareness involves becoming more conscious of our thoughts, feelings and behaviours. It helps us gain perspective and reframe our view of the situation before us, leading to new insights and solutions.

One way to do this is by temporarily shifting our focus away from the problematic situation. Moving focus might be a creative distraction, allowing our minds to rest and recharge. Then, we re-approach the problem with fresh eyes and a new perspective.

Through this process, we either find a new approach to the current problem or improve future performance by learning from our experiences. It's similar to Viktor Frankl's idea of finding meaning and purpose in the face of adversity [87], and using that perspective to transcend our circumstances.

Inputs

Finally, *controlling inputs* completes the golden triangle. Being overwhelmed by too much information is a significant leadership challenge. Such overload is especially prevalent in VUCA environments with wicked problems.

Here are some ways to control inputs to manage the flow of information:

- Establish clear priorities for your team and yourself, which helps you focus on the most critical information and filter out distractions.

- Clearly define the scope of the wicked problem you're trying to address, which helps you narrow your focus and avoid getting side-tracked by irrelevant information.

- Use technology to help you manage the flow of information. For example, you might set up email or social media filters, use project management tools to organise information, or data visualisation tools to make complex information more digestible.

- Establish clear communication channels with your team and your stakeholders, which helps ensure that information is communicated promptly and organised, reducing the risk of information overload.

- Delegate tasks and responsibilities effectively to avoid taking on too much yourself, which helps distribute the workload and ensures adequate information management.

Building on your personality and character strengths

Your personality and its interaction with your character strengths are the foundation of psychological performance. From this base, your mindset develops, allowing you to achieve mental toughness and the ability to flow.

The HEXACO personality test delineates four personality types based on six traits: honesty-humility, emotionality or neuroticism, extroversion, agreeableness, conscientiousness and openness [47].

1 **Average** people, the most common personality type, are high in neuroticism and extroversion while low in openness.

2 **Reserved** types are emotionally stable but not open or neurotic; they are not particularly extroverted but are somewhat agreeable and conscientious.

3 **Role models** score low in neuroticism and high in all the other traits. They are dependable and open to new ideas.

4 **Self-centred** people score very high in extroversion and below average in openness, agreeableness, and conscientiousness.

Authentic leaders fit the Role Model personality type. They're empathic, strong characters who are difficult to intimidate, stay calm in the face of challenges, and refuse to accept lies, untruths or dissimulation. They're who you want in your corner when a wicked problem arises.

Wicked leaders seek to understand their character strengths and grow from that understanding [95-97]. Recent research shows that when you understand and activate your character strengths, you become more resilient, better able to manage negative stress, and more readily able to change your mindset, be mindful and access flow, boosting your broader well-being [95-97].

The Values in Action (VIA) classification of character strengths is a scientifically valid classification of twenty-four character strengths distributed across six virtues (Figure 7) [98]. To these, I've added the foundational virtue of physiological wellness.

7.	TRANSCENDENCE	APPRECIATION | GRATITUDE | HOPE | HUMOUR | SPIRITUALITY
6.	TEMPERANCE	FORGIVENESS | HUMILITY | PRUDENCE | SELF-REGULATION
5.	JUSTICE	TEAMWORK | FAIRNESS | LEADERSHIP
4.	HUMANITY	LOVE | KINDNESS | SOCIAL INTELLIGENCE
3.	COURAGE	BRAVERY | PERSEVERANCE | HONESTY | ZEST
2.	WISDOM	CREATIVITY | CURIOSITY | JUDGMENT | LOVE OF LEARNING | PERSPECTIVE
1.	WELLNESS	PHYSIOLOGICAL STRENGTHS

FIGURE 7 Values in Action plus

Importantly, we cycle through different virtues across life. Hence, the ranking of our character strengths varies across our lives, and our 'positioning' within these virtues shifts accordingly. A friend recently told me, 'No one changes,' but he's wrong: people *can* change, depending on their mindset.

Developing a growth mindset

Carol Dweck identifies two mindsets: fixed and growth [99]. People with a fixed mindset have a deterministic view of the world. They believe their intelligence is static, leading to a desire to look smart and avoid challenges. As a result, they give up easily, ignore helpful criticism, and feel threatened by the success of others. People with a fixed mindset tend to plateau early and achieve less than their full potential. Fixed mindsets do not enable wicked problem-solving.

By contrast, people with a growth mindset have a greater sense of free will [99], believing they can further develop their intelligence. A growth mindset leads to a desire to learn and embrace challenges. You persist in the face of failure, see effort as the route to mastery, learn from criticism, and find lessons and inspiration in the success of others. People with a growth mindset are perpetually learning from their own experiences and the experiences of others.

Developing a growth mindset requires several strategies, including:

1   **Embrace challenges.** Rather than shying away from complex or unfamiliar tasks, individuals with a growth mindset embrace them as opportunities for learning and growth. Furthermore, they recognise that tackling challenging tasks leads to new skills and insights.

2   **Persist through obstacles.** Individuals with a growth mindset understand that setbacks and obstacles are inevitable in the learning process. Therefore, rather than giving up when faced with difficulties, they persist through challenges and use them as opportunities to learn and grow.

3   **Seek out feedback.** Individuals with a growth mindset actively seek feedback from others and use it to improve their skills and abilities.

4   **Cultivate a love of learning.** Individuals with a growth mindset are motivated by a love of learning and a desire to improve continuously.

Stress states and mental toughness

Mental toughness is your ability to cope with stressors, pressure and challenges. Commonly, we conceive of stressors purely negatively. However, my mentor, psychologist and leadership expert Wilf Jarvis [100] distinguishes between *eustress* and *distress*.

Eustress refers to positive stress, or stress that is beneficial or motivating. It is associated with feelings of excitement, challenge and satisfaction, and is often related to personal growth, achievement or success. For example, starting a new job, preparing for a presentation or training for a marathon can all be sources of eustress. These situations may be challenging, but they can also be perceived as opportunities for growth and development.

Eustress has positive physiological effects on the body. When we experience eustress, our bodies release a swathe of hormones (endorphins, dopamine, serotonin, adrenaline and oxytocin) that help us to feel more energised and focused. Eustress also improves our immune system and enhances our cognitive functioning. However, it is essential to note that eustress can still be stressful, and excessive eustress leads to burnout or other adverse outcomes. Therefore, it is crucial to manage eustress effectively by setting realistic goals, practising self-care and seeking support when needed.

Distress refers to negative stress, i.e., stress that is harmful or overwhelming and detrimental to physical and mental health. Distress arises from various situations, such as financial problems, relationship difficulties, health issues or work-related stress. When we experience distress, we may feel anxious, irritable or overwhelmed. These feelings have adverse effects on our mood, behaviour and relationships.

Distress also has adverse physiological effects on the body. For example, when we experience distress, our bodies release stress hormones (cortisol, adrenaline, corticotropic-releasing hormone, adrenocorticotropic hormone) that lead to increased heart rate, blood pressure and respiration. Over time, these physiological responses may contribute to the development of chronic health problems such as heart disease, diabetes and depression. Therefore, it is vital to manage distress effectively by practising stress-management techniques such as meditation, deep breathing or exercise. In addition, seeking social support, setting realistic goals and practising self-care also help reduce distress and improve overall well-being.

I should note that the body's response to stress, whether eustress or distress, is part of its survival mechanism, which is often referred to as the 'fight-or-flight' response. This response prepares the body to either confront or flee from potential harm, and it involves several physiological changes that are largely mediated by hormones.

When a stressor is perceived, the brain activates the adrenal glands to release hormones such as adrenaline (epinephrine) and cortisol. These hormones cause several changes in the body, such as increased heart rate, blood pressure and glucose levels, which help the body prepare to respond to the stressor.

In the case of eustress, these hormones help to energise and motivate individuals to tackle the challenging or exciting situation at hand. The release of these hormones in response to positive stressors can enhance performance and promote feelings of excitement and satisfaction. In the case of distress, the same hormones are released, but the context and the individual's perception of the situation are different. Rather than feeling motivated or excited, the individual may feel overwhelmed, anxious or fearful. Prolonged release of these hormones due to chronic distress can lead to negative health effects, such as anxiety, depression, heart disease and other stress-related disorders.

Essentially, it's not only the hormones themselves, but also the context, the individual's perception and interpretation of the situation, and the duration of the stress that determine whether the stress is beneficial (eustress) or harmful (distress).

The term 'stress state' refers to the physiological and psychological response of the body to any demand placed upon it, whether that's a physical threat or emotional challenge. This state is intended to help the organism survive and adapt to changing circumstances, and is largely mediated by the nervous and endocrine systems, which work together to prepare the body to respond to the perceived demand or threat.

Both eustress and distress are types of stress states but, as we've seen, they have different effects on the body and mind. The important thing to remember is that the perception and interpretation of the stressor (whether it's viewed as a challenge or a threat) and the individual's capacity to cope with the stressor play a crucial role in determining whether a stress state will be eustress or distress. The same stressor might provoke eustress in one person and distress in another, depending on their individual perceptions, experiences and coping abilities. Hence, managing our stress state is not only about managing the stressors themselves, but also our perceptions and responses to them.

The number of stressors and the personal resources available to cope with them significantly influence your stress state. Stressors indeed represent a demand on your resources, requiring time, energy, attention, and potentially even material resources to manage. Depending on the nature of the stressor and the personal resources at hand, this can lead to a state of eustress or distress.

The quantity and quality of personal resources play a crucial role in managing and responding to stressors. For example, someone with high mental toughness may perceive a challenging situation not as a threat, but as an opportunity for growth, leading to a state of eustress. Similarly, having sufficient time, knowledge or support from others can help effectively manage stressors.

Understanding this interplay between stressors and personal resources provides a foundation for building resilience and mental toughness. Mental toughness, characterised by resilience, confidence, and the ability to manage pressure, is a key factor in determining how we interpret and respond to stressors.

The stronger our mental toughness, the better we can respond to life's challenges, turning potential distress into eustress and adversity into opportunity. This is why developing mental toughness is such an integral part of managing stress and promoting overall mental well-being. In the following section, I dig deeper into the concept of mental toughness, its components, and how it can be cultivated to enhance our ability to navigate through life's stressors.

According to Doug Strycharczyk and Peter Clough, mental toughness is a product of four key concepts—what they call the 'four Cs model' – which have important roles to play in taming wicked problems [101]:

1 **Challenge.** Individuals with high mental toughness view challenges not as overwhelming obstacles, but as opportunities for learning and growth. They approach difficult situations with curiosity and enthusiasm, continuously seeking out new experiences to stretch their abilities. In the context of wicked problems—complex issues with no straightforward solutions, like climate change or social inequality—this translates to an ability to embrace uncertainty, see value in complexity, and use these challenges as learning opportunities.

2 **Confidence,** both in oneself and in one's interactions with others, is crucial for mental toughness. This involves having a strong belief in one's abilities and decisions, as well as confidence in influencing people and events. For wicked problems, this could mean having confidence in one's ability to contribute to solutions, and confidence in collaborative efforts to tackle these complex issues.

3 **Commitment** refers to a person's ability to carry through with tasks and goals, even in the face of difficulty. People with high mental toughness

show perseverance and determination. In terms of wicked problems, these manifest themselves in the ability to stay dedicated to solving these complex issues, despite the many setbacks and roadblocks that may arise.

4 **Control** involves the belief that one has the power to shape one's own destiny and manage one's emotions, rather than feeling powerless or overly influenced by external events. This aspect of mental toughness allows individuals to maintain composure and focus under pressure. When dealing with wicked problems, this could manifest as maintaining emotional balance in the face of daunting challenges and believing in one's agency to effect change.

By understanding and cultivating these 'four Cs' of mental toughness, individuals can better manage stressors, converting potentially harmful distress into productive eustress. In the face of wicked problems, this means not only surviving, but thriving amidst complexity and uncertainty, transforming challenges into opportunities for growth, innovation and positive change.

Lifelong learning

Lifelong learning refers to the ongoing, voluntary and self-motivated pursuit of knowledge for personal or professional development throughout an individual's life. It emphasises the importance of continuous learning from a variety of sources—including formal education, self-study, workshops, online courses, seminars and mentoring—but especially from formative, real-world experiences [102, 103].

Lifelong learning is crucial for leaders, especially in the context of taming wicked problems, for several reasons:

1   **Nature of wicked problems.** Wicked problems are complex, multifaceted, and often resist typical problem-solving approaches. They evolve over time and can be ambiguous in nature. As such, leaders must continuously learn, adapt and apply novel strategies to address them effectively.

2   **Dynamic environments.** The world is rapidly changing, with technology, globalisation and socio-political shifts regularly altering the landscape. Lifelong learning ensures leaders stay up to speed with these shifts, allowing them to navigate and adjust to the evolving nature of wicked problems.

3   **Diverse perspectives.** Lifelong learning exposes leaders to a variety of perspectives, disciplines and cultures. This broadened worldview equips them with a more holistic understanding of wicked problems, promoting cross-disciplinary solutions and collaborative approaches.

4   **Flexibility and adaptability.** Continuous learning helps make leaders more receptive to change,

more resilient in the face of setbacks, and more agile in their decision-making processes—all essential traits for tackling wicked problems.

5 **Building trust.** Leaders who are seen as continually growing and adapting are often more respected and considered more credible within their organisation and community, especially when seeking buy-in for innovative solutions to complex challenges.

6 **Skill enhancement.** Wicked problems often require a blend of soft and hard skills, from empathetic communication to data analytics. Lifelong learning ensures that leaders continuously refine and expand their skill sets to meet these diverse demands.

In summary, to effectively address wicked problems, leaders must be committed to continuous growth, adaptation and knowledge acquisition. Lifelong learning is not just a tool, but a growth mindset that empowers leaders to navigate the complexities of our modern world.

CONCLUSION: ARE YOU SORTED?

The six SORTED principles of Situation, Objective, Reality, Template, Execution and Development provide a comprehensive framework for taming wicked problems and taking wicked opportunities.

By sharpening our situation awareness, defining purposeful goals, assessing reality with critical thinking, templating possible solutions, executing the most promising solution with a bias for action, and improving our solution and wicked problem-solving skills, we can foster a resilient style of leadership and build reliably safe organisations that are better equipped to deal with future wicked problems and seize wicked opportunities.

This style of leadership, which I call *wicked leadership*, involves a continuous process of learning, adaptation and improvement, and emphasises the importance of individual and organisational learning as critical drivers of success. By embracing this approach, we can overcome even the most complex challenges and emerge stronger and more effective.

Finally, *you cannot and should not take on wicked problems or opportunities by yourself*. Coaching is crucial to adopting the principles of taming wicked problems because it provides individuals with personalised guidance and support as they develop and apply their skills in practice.

Coaching helps individuals identify their strengths and weaknesses, set clear goals and develop a plan for achieving them. Coaches also provide feedback and support as individuals apply the principles in real-world situations, helping them navigate challenges and adjust as needed.

Coaching also helps foster a culture of continuous learning and improvement within an organisation. By providing coaching to individuals at all levels of the organisation, leaders can encourage a shared commitment to ongoing growth and development, and create an environment in which everyone invests in improving their wicked problem-solving skills.

Furthermore, coaching helps individuals develop the resilience and adaptability needed to navigate complex and unpredictable situations. By providing individuals with the tools and support they need to overcome challenges and embrace change, coaching can help create a more agile and responsive organisation better equipped to deal with wicked problems and opportunities.

My closing challenge to you is to ask yourself:

* What's the most difficult problem or opportunity you face right now?

* What's your situational awareness of that problem or opportunity?

* What do you want to achieve relating to it?

* What's the reality of your situation? No, *really.*

* Do you have a plan?

* Are you ready to act?

* How's your skill set?

In short—are you **SORTED**?

Connect With Me and Unleash Your Leadership Potential

OVER MORE THAN thirty years, I've helped equip countless professionals with knowledge and skills to transform challenges into stepping stones, walking alongside them as they experienced taming wicked problems and leveraging wicked opportunities of many different kinds. Drawing from those experiences, as well as research and professional practice in leadership, strategy, and risk and crisis management, I've sought to hone the art of fostering *Clarity*, *Confidence* and *Performance*:

- Clarity. Cut through noise with enhanced communication and streamlined decisions.

- Confidence. Overcome imposter syndrome and self-doubt in order to lead with authenticity.

- Performance. Boost productivity, innovate, and ensure collective success.

Whether you're an aspiring or a seasoned leader, I'm excited to work with you to elevate your potential.

Discover more at clivesmallman.com, or connect with me at clive@clivesmallman.com.

To *wicked* leadership,
CLIVE

References

1. Lovell, J. and J. Kluger, Apollo 13. 1995: Coronet.
2. Simon, H.A., The Sciences of the Artificial. Third ed. 1996, Cambridge, MA: The MIT Press.
3. Rittel, H.W.J. and M.M. Webber, Dilemmas in a general theory of planning. Policy Sciences, 1973. 4(2): p. 155-169.
4. Pearson, C.M. and I.I. Mitroff, From crisis prone to crisis prepared: A framework for crisis management. Academy of Management Executive, 1993. 7(1): p. 48-59.
5. Klasche, B., After COVID-19: What can we learn about wicked problem governance? Social Sciences and Humanities, Open, 2021. 4.
6. Moon, M.J., Fighting against COVID-19 with agility, transparency, and participation: Wicked policy problems and new governance challenges. Public Administration Review, 2020. 80(4): p. 651-656.
7. Peters, G.B., What is so wicked about wicked problems? A conceptual analysis and a research program. Policy and Society, 2017. 36(3): p. 385-396.
8. Snowden, D.J. and M.E. Boone, A leader's framework for decision making. Harvard Business Review, 2007. 85(11): p. 68-76.
9. Turnbull, N. and R. Hoppe, Problematizing 'wicked-ness: A critique of the wicked problems concept from philosophy to practice. Policy and Society, 2019. 38(2): p. 315-337.
10. HSE, The Fire at Hickson & Welch Limited. A report of the investigation by the Health and Safety Executive into

the fatal fire at Hickson & Welch Limited, Castleford on
21 September 1992. 1994: Health and Safety Executive.

11. Shrivastava, P., et al., Understanding industrial crises.
     Journal of Management Studies, 1988. 25(4): p. 283-303.

12. United States Congress, Final Report of the Select
     Committee to Investigate the January 6th Attack on the
     United States Capitol. 2022: U.S.Government Publishing
     Office.

13. Labov, W., Sociolinguistic Patterns. 1972, Philadelphia:
     University of Pennsylvania Press.

14. Gigerenzer, G., Gut Feelings. The Intelligence of the
     Unconscious. 2007, London: Penguin Allen Lane.

15. Lewis, M., The Big Short: Inside the Doomsday Machine.
     2010: W. W. Norton & Company.

16. Stead, E.M. and C. Smallman, Understanding business
     failures: learning and unlearning lessons from industrial
     crises. Journal of Contingencies and Crisis Management,
     1999. 7(1): p. 1-18.

17. Turner, B.A. and N. Pidgeon, Man-Made Disasters.
     Second ed. 1997, Oxford: Butterworth-Heinemann.

18. Arrhenius, S., On the influence of carbonic acid in the
     air upon the temperature of the ground. The London,
     Edinburgh, and Dublin Philosophical Magazine and
     Journal of Science, 1896. 41(251): p. 237-276.

19. Fleming, J.R., The Callendar Effect. The Life and Work
     of Guy Stewart Callendar (1898–1964), the Scientist
     Who Established the Carbon Dioxide Theory of Climate
     Change. 2007: American Meteorological Society.

20. Endsley, M.R., Measurement of situation awareness in
     dynamic systems. Human Factors, 1995. 37(1): p. 65-84.

21. Endsley, M.R., Toward a theory of situation awareness in
     dynamic systems. Human Factors, 1995. 37(1): p. 32-64.

22. Bandura, A., Social Foundations of Thought and Action:
     a Social Cognitive Theory. 1986, Englewood Cliffs, NJ:
     Prentice-Hall.

23. Church, M., S. Coburn and C. Fink, Speakership: The Art of Oration, the Science of Influence. 2015, Balgowlah, NSW: Thought Leaders Publishing.

24. Csikszentmihalyi, M., Flow. The Psychology of Optimal Experience. 2008, New York: HarperCollins.

25. Udemy, Workplace Distraction report. 2018: Udemy for Business.

26. Covey, S.R.W., The Seven Habits of Highly Effective People. 1989: Free Press.

27. Church, A.H., M. Del Giudice and A. Margulies, All that glitters is not gold: Maximizing the impact of executive assessment and development efforts. Leadership & Organization Development Journal,, 2017. 38(6): p. 765-779.

28. Roth, E.M., J. Multer and T. Raslear, Shared situation awareness as a contributor to high reliability performance in railroad operations. Organization Studies, 2006. 27(7): p. 967-988.

29. Rochlin, G.I., T.R. La Porte and K.H. Roberts, The self-designing high-reliability organisation: Aircraft carrier flight operations at sea. Naval War College Review, 1987. 40(4): p. 76-90.

30. Osterwalder, A. and Y. Pigneur, Business Model Generation: A Handbook for Visionaries, Game Changers, and Challengers. 2010, Chichester: John Wiley and Sons.

31. Curedale, R., Empathy Maps: Step-by-Step Guide. 2019: Design Community College Inc.

32. Ashcroft, J., The Lego Case Study. 2014: John Ashcroft and Company.

33. Robertson, D. and B. Breen, Brick by Brick: How LEGO Rewrote the Rules of Innovation and Conquered the Global Toy Industry. 2014: Century - Trade.

34. Hastings, R. and E. Meyer, No Rules Rules: Netflix and the Culture of Reinvention. 2020: Penguin.

35. Fox, L., Enron: the Rise and Fall. 2003, Hoboken NJ: John Wiley and Sons, Inc.

36. Pruzan, P., From control to values-based management and accountability. Journal of Business Ethics, 1998. 17: p. 1379-1394.

37. Locke, E.A. and G.P. Latham, A Theory of Goal Setting and Task Performance. 1990, Englewood Cliffs, NJ: Prentice Hall.

38. Stajkovic, A.D., E.A. Locke and E.S. Blair, A first examination of the relationships between primed subconscious goals, assigned conscious goals, and task performance. Journal of Applied Psychology, 2006. 91: p. 1172-1180.

39. Collins, J. and J.I. Porras, Built to Last. Successful Habit of Visionary Companies. Second ed. 2004, New York: HarperCollins.

40. United Nations, Transforming Our World: The 2030 Agenda for Sustainable Development (A/RES/70/1). 2015: United Nations, Department of Economic and Social Affairs, Sustainable Development.

41. McChesney, C., S. Covey and J. Huling, The 4 Disciplines of Execution. 2012, New York: Free Press.

42. Miller, G.A., The magical number seven, plus or minus two: Some limits on our capacity for processing information. Psychological Review, 1956. 63: p. 81-97.

43. Purves, D., et al., eds. Neuroscience. Sixth ed. 2018, Oxford University Press: New York.

44. Chouinard, Y. and V. Stanley, The Responsible Company: What We've Learned from Patagonia's First 40 Years. 2012: Patagonia Books.

45. Unilever, Unilever Sustainable Living Plan 2010 to 2020: Summary of 10 years' progress. 2021: Unilever.

46. Unilever. The Unilever Compass for Sustianble Growth. 2020 19 August 2023]; Available from: https://www .unilever.com/files/8f9a3825-2101-411f-9a31-7e6f1763 93a4/the-unilever-compass.pdf.

47. Daft, R.L. and D. Marcic, Understanding Management. 12th ed. 2022: Cengage Learning.
48. Bristol Royal Infirmary Inquiry, The Inquiry into the management of care of children receiving complex heart surgery at the Bristol Royal Infirmary. Interim report: Removal and retention of human material. 2000, The Stationery Office: London.
49. Fraher, A.L., A toxic triangle of destructive leadership at Bristol Royal Infirmary: A study of organisational Munchausen syndrome by proxy. Leadership, 2014. 12(1): p. 34-52.
50. Plato, Early Socratic Dialogues. 2005: Penguin.
51. Janis, I.L., Victims of Groupthink: Psychological Study of Foreign-Policy Decisions and Fiascoes. 1972, Boston: Houghton Mifflin.
52. Janis, I.L., Groupthink: Psychological Studies of Policy Decisions and Fiascoes. 1982: Houghton Mifflin.
53. Staw, B.M., Knee-deep in the big muddy: A study of escalating commitment to a chosen course of action. Organisational Behaviour and Human Performance, 1976. 16: p. 27-44.
54. Staw, B.M., The escalation of commitment: an update and appraisal, in Organisational Decision Making, Z. Shapira, Editor. 1997, Cambridge University Press. p. 191-215.
55. Ross, J. and B.M. Staw, Organisational escalation and exit: lessons from the Shoreham nuclear power plant. Academy of Management Journal, 1993. 36(4): p. 701-732.
56. Staw, B.M. and J. Ross, Understanding escalation situations: antecedents, prototypes and solutions, in Research in Organisational Behaviour, B.M. Staw and L.L. Cummings, Editors. 1987, JAI Press. p. 39-78.
57. Mintz, A. and C. Wayne, The Polythink Syndrome: U. S. Foreign Policy Decisions on 9/11, Afghanistan, Iraq, Iran,

Syria, and ISIS. 2016, Palo Alto: Stanford University Press.

58. Lundberg, A., Successful with the Agile Spotify Framework: Squads, Tribes and Chapters - The Next Step After Scrum and Kanban? 2020: Books On Demand.

59. Catmull, E., Creativity, Inc.: Overcoming the Unseen Forces That Stand in the Way of True Inspiration. Second ed. 2023, London: Transworld Publishers.

60. Catmull, E., How Pixar fosters collective creativity. Harvard Business Review, 2008(August).

61. Cullen, The Ladbroke Grove Rail Inquiry Part 1 Report. 2000, Her Majesty's Stationery Office: Norwich.

62. Law, J. Ladbroke Grove, Or How to Think about Failing Systems. 2003 6 December 2003 [cited 2005 18 July]; Available from: http://www.comp.lancs.ac.uk/sociology/papers/Law-Ladbroke-Grove-Failing-Systems.pdf.

63. Gawande, A., The Checklist Manifesto: How to Get Things Right. 2009: Metropolitan Books.

64. Knight, G. and C. Smallman, Crisis response: aligning scripts and actors, in Sixth International Symposium on Process Organization Studies - Organization Routines: How they are created, maintained and changed. 2014: Rhodes, Greece.

65. Pearson, C.M. and I.I. Mitroff, Crisis Management: A Diagnostic Guide for Improving Your Organization's Crisis-Preparedness. 1993: Wiley.

66. Smith, P., Cyber experts worry as Medibank puts hack behind it, in Financial Review. 2023.

67. Kottler, S., February 28th DDoS Incident Report, in GitHub Blog. 2018.

68. Dodge v. Ford Motor Co.,. 1919, Michigan Supreme Ct.

69. Earl, S. and S. Waddington, Brand Vandals: Reputation Wreckers and How to Build Better Defences. Kindle ed. 2013, London: Bloomsbury.

70. Fowler, S., Whistleblower: My Journey to Silicon Valley and Fight for Justice at Uber. 2020: Viking.
71. Khojasteh, Y., ed. Supply Chain Risk Management: Advanced Tools, Models, and Developments. 2017, Springer.
72. Clausewitz, C.v., On War. Revised ed. 183²/1989: Princeton University Press.
73. Peters, T.J. and R.H. Waterman, In Search of Excellence: Lessons from America's Best-Run Companies. 1982, New York: Harper Business.
74. Peters, T.J., The Excellence Dividend: Principles for Prospering in Turbulent Times from a Lifetime in Pursuit of Excellence. 2018, New York: Nicholas Brealey Publishing.
75. Bossidy, L. and R. Charan, Execution: the Discipline of Getting Things Done. Second ed. 2009, New York: Crown Business.
76. Bruch, H. and S. Ghosal, A Bias for Action: How Effective Managers Harness Their Willpower, Achieve Results, and Stop Wasting Time. 2004, Cambridge, MA: Harvard Business Review Press.
77. Scott, S., Fierce Conversations: Achieving Success at Work and in Life One Conversation at a Time. Second ed. 2017, London: Penguin Random House.
78. Schlosser, E., Fast Food Nation: The Dark Side of the All-American Meal. 2012: Mariner Books.
79. Spurlock, M., Don't Eat This Book: Fast Food and the Supersizing of America. 2006: Berkley.
80. CAWS, Helping McDonald's Realize Its ESG Potential: Investor Presentation. 2022: The Coalition for Corporate Accountability of Animal Welfare and Sustainability.
81. Meyer, M., Permanent failure and the failure of organisational performance, in When Things Go Wrong. Organisational Failures and Breakdowns, H.K. Anheier,

Editor. 1999, Sage Publications Ltd: London. p. 197-212.

82. Oakland, J.S., R.J. Oakland and M.A. Turner, Total Quality Management and Operational Excellence: Text with Cases. Fifth ed. 2021, Abingdon: Routledge.

83. Christensen, C.M., The Innovator's Dilemma: When New Technologies Cause Great Firms to Fail. Second ed. 2000: Harvard Business Review Press.

84. Christensen, C.M., The Innovator's Solution: Creating and Sustaining Successful Growth. 2013: Harvard Business Review Press.

85. Barrett, F.J., Yes to the Mess. Surprising Leadership Lessons from Jazz. 2012: Harvard Business Review Press.

86. Edmondson, A.C., Psychological safety and learning behaviour in work teams. Administrative Science Quarterly, 1999. 44(2): p. 350-383.

87. Frankl, V.E., Man's Search for Meaning. An Introduction to Logotherapy. 4th ed. 1992, Boston, MA: Beacon.

88. Frankl, V.E., On the Theory and Therapy of Mental Disorders. An Introduction to Logotherapy and Existential Analysis. 2004, New York NY: Brunner-Routledge.

89. Bunting, M., The Mindful Leader. 7 Practices for Transforming Your Leadership, Your Organisation and Your Life. 2016, Milton, QLD: John Wiley & Sons.

90. Edwards, A., The DNA of Performance. How to Unlock Your Genes for Unstoppable Energy and Vitality. 2020, Melbourne: alessandraedwards.com.

91. Stanley, N., How to Sleep Well. The Science of Sleeping Smarter, Living Better and Being Productive. 2018, Chichester: Capstone/John Wiley and Sons.

92. Noakes, M. and P. Clifton, The CSIRO Total Wellbeing Diet. 2005, Camberwell, Vic: Penguin Books/CSIRO.

93. Eurich, T., What self-awareness really is (and how to cultivate it). Harvard Business Review, 2018. Digital article.

94. Kahneman, D., Thinking, Fast and Slow. 2011, New York: Macmillan.

95. Peterson, C. and M.E.P. Seligman, Character Strengths and Virtues: a Handbook and Classification. 2004, Washington, DC and New York, NY: American Psychological Association and Oxford Universty Press.

96. Niemiec, R.M., Character Strengths Interventions. A Field Guide for Practitioners. 2018, Boston, MA: Hogrefe.

97. Niemiec, R.M. and R.E. McGrath, The Power of Character Strengths. Appreciate and Ignite Your Positive Personality. 2019, Cincinnati, OH: VIA Institute on Character.

98. Seligman, M.E.P., et al., Positive psychology progress: empirical validation of interventions. American Psychologist, 2005. 60(5): p. 410-421.

99. Dweck, C.S., Mindset. The New Psychology of Success. Second ed. 2007, New York: Penguin Random House.

100. Jarvis, W., Four Quadrant Leadership (Stage One). Ninth ed. 2004, Cupertino, CA: The Wilfred Jarvis Institute.

101. Clough, P. and D. Strycharczyk, Developing Mental Toughness. Coaching Strategies to Improve Performance, Resilience and Wellbeing. 2015, London: Kogan Page.

102. Kolb, D.A., Experiential Learning: Experience as the Source of Learning and Development. Second ed. 2015, Upper Saddle River, NJ: Pearson Education, Inc.

103. Heath, C. and D. Heath, The Power of Moments. Why Certain Experiences Have Extraordinary Impact. 2017, London: Corgi.

Acknowledgements

M Y DEEPEST gratitude to Chris Freeman for his friendship, wisdom and brotherly love, and for helping restore my life by design.

Many thanks to Professor Peter Ryan for his friendship and patient, highly knowledgeable and skilled mentorship and support in a business marred by unnecessarily adversarial regulation.

Jeanine Hind, my friend and student, is an inspiration, proving you're never old enough not to learn new tricks.

Mario Bekes, for showing how to thrive in work-life, even when you get lemons thrown your way.

To James Michael, thanks for rekindling our conversation about leadership and culture and showing the way to success in thought leadership.

At Thought Leaders Business School, thank you to Matt Church for the genial, gently brutal, yet beautiful candour that gave birth to this book. A 'love note' to Lisa O'Neill for fabulous, relentless, wicked leadership by example through a period of deep wickedness. Thank you, Dr Isabella Allan, for helping me navigate the wicked world and reminding me one can only tame, not solve, wicked problems.

Thank you, Anna Stanford, for finding and communicating a 'contained, controlled sense of magic and beautiful chaos' (her words) in and among my ramblings and translating it into a brand and website.

At Dent Global, thanks to Glen Carlson and Mike Reid for offering structure and demanding ruthlessly consistent clarity in the 5 'Ps'.

To Andrew Tracy (my highly skilled, creative and patient editor), Scott MacMillan (my publisher), Carolyn Jackson and Ania Ziemirska at Grammar Factory, many thanks for navigating the disorder of my writing, taming my manuscript, and designing this beautiful book. Coping with a mid-course fundamental change of direction was not easy, I know.

Thanks to Anton Harrison-Kern, Charlene Matabuena and Alexandra Almendas for levelling me up.

Love to Christos Haropoulou-Smallman for exemplifying and communicating sales mastery.

And to Nikos Haropoulos-Smallman, love and gratitude for demonstrating that saying 'yes' to the mess is nearly always beautiful.

Much love for mum, June Smallman, aged ninety-two at the time of writing, for unwittingly providing the germ of an idea when she told me in early 2022 that this was the most dangerous time she could remember since 1945.

Love to my sister, Dr Jane Smallman, and brother-in-law Dr William Allsop, solvers of wicked problems in harbours, ports and estuaries worldwide.

Love to my brother-in-law Andreas Haropoulos and my Greek family, all suffering the ravages of the climate crisis as I write.

Saving the best for last: all my love to my long-suffering wife, Dr Mary Haropoulou, for forty years of love, patience and understanding. She is too often the calm eye in my chaotic creative storm.

CLIVE SMALLMAN

August 2023, Salamander Bay, NSW, Australia

About the author
Clive Smallman PhD

LOOKING BACK, Clive's adult life started with a wicked problem: he failed high school.

His plans of studying geography or oceanography at a top university were torn up in the space of three letters printed on his high school examination results: 'D E O'. 'D' and 'E' explain themselves; 'O' signifies he didn't even make it to the advanced grades, and was also the shape his mouth made when reading said results.

Having blotted his copybook so spectacularly, Clive became and remains a serial student, culminating in a PhD in operational risk management. He is also a serial student of 'wickedness', having researched, taught and mentored in the space of risk and crisis management for over thirty years. Clive couples that expertise with an earlier career in artificial intelligence, where he applied machine learning to such wicked problems as tomato plant disease diagnosis, adaptive battlefield technology and gas well analysis.

Clive specialises in equipping executive leaders to tame wicked individual and organisational problems and leverage opportunities through improved critical thinking and creative problem-solving. He aims to develop deep insight into clients' challenges, generating clarity, reducing friction, and enabling purposeful, transformative action.

What sets Clive apart?

- He is the CEO of a higher education start-up, independent director of another two, and independent director of a charity addressing wicked problems in the developing world

- Recent experience of advisory work in a difficult regulatory environment

- Experience of large-scale change management and leading large, complex, spatially dispersed organisations

- Thirty years of research, education, mentoring, coaching and training in risk and crisis management, culminating in the conferral of the title Professor Emeritus

- Honours degree with a climatology specialism (now there's a wicked problem!), master's degree in artificial intelligence, PhD in operational risk management, and a Cambridge research fellow in health, safety and environmental management

- Trained in negotiation at Harvard; in positive psychology at the University of California, Berkeley; in design thinking with IDEO; and received Master Coach training from the Life Coaching Academy

- Worked on taming wicked problems with major brands such as GEC (now Ericsson and Siemens), Centrica, Aviva, Ford, and Coca-Cola

www.ingramcontent.com/pod-product-compliance
Lightning Source LLC
Chambersburg PA
CBHW031846200326
41597CB00012B/292